THE ART OF LIVING

MrJames LifeCoach
The Art of Living

Published by Spines
ISBN: 978-965-578-998-0

THE ART OF LIVING

WISDOM FROM PROVERBS

REMEMBER F.R.O.G.

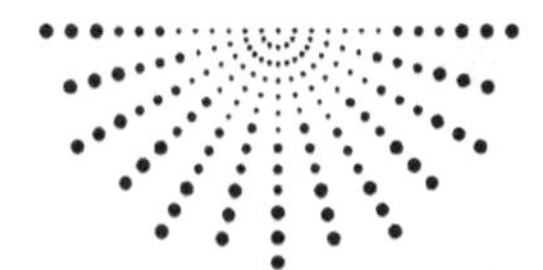

MRJAMES LIFECOACH

CONTENTS

PREFACE

It is not within the author's authority, nor his intention, to speak neither for nor against the doctrines, principles, concepts, or tenets of any Church. Therefore, as the author discusses his personal beliefs and real-life experiences, the comments by the V and the entirety of the information are to be regarded as his interpretation of the material presented. The author, therefore, assumes all responsibility for its content.

ACKNOWLEDGMENTS

The author takes this opportunity to express sincere thanks to God, and gratitude for the enlightenment received from his journey through addiction, jails, rehabs, grief, pain, divorce, disappointments, relapse, abstinence, the rooms of recovery, and the recovery process. He is equally thankful for the many prayers offered on his behalf by his x-wife, Angelia; their daughter, Darnaisha; two sons, Devin and Darrell Jr.; and three granddaughters: Trinity, Mariah, and Morgan. MrJames owes and attributes the inspiration to complete this volume to two nephews: Riki and Juan, and his youngest brother, Karl (aka Shorty, K.C., Short Coat).

In the final days of constructing this art of living lesson from Proverbs literary work, my nephew Juan said to me, "Unc, you got to keep it simple. Everybody did not go to college. Sometimes I have to use a dictionary to understand you." My other nephew Ricki reminds me of myself as a young man. I was eager, excited, and searching for real-life truths. After coming to the place in my life, and in the art of living, where I was sick and tired of being sick and tired; exhausted from being my own worst enemy; and being used and abused by life; it was then that I began to "seek, knock, and ask" for Godly wisdom.

However, spending a few days with Riki has reminded me of what I felt like; and what it feels like inside when the proverbial "**student is ready,**" but the teacher did not appear. I am grateful for the whisper of the still soft voice of Grandma, who was my teacher every day of her life until the day she died. The first time I heard her inaudible still soft voice was shortly after that day. I was seeking answers to my questions about the art of living without grandma in my life anymore.

I am reminded of the first time I felt those feelings, and while reflecting on those days of the past and preparing this work, I can hear her inaudible voice whispering to me from the eternal realm: "Baby, do YOU remember how YOU felt when the teacher did not appear?" That memory is never to be forgotten by MrJames, as he recalls the days of the F.R.O.G.S. dilemma in his life, and before it was time for him to know his grandma was his real- time, real-life ever-present teacher in the art of living.

Now, MrJames appreciates and is fully aware Grandma was responsible for preparing him for his life mission; even from the eternal realm she remains his art of living teacher. He knows that she knows his life purposes, and he knows the importance The Book of Proverbs is to filling his divine life mission. It is a treasure chest and a storage place for the "essential" elements needed by readers, in order to produce profound positive outcomes; in the art of living as a reflection of the divine blueprint; and to the full measure of the preordained and divinely created life purpose.Therefore, as my brother Karl might say to me, "handle your business, Brother," I express sincere heartfelt gratitude to Grandma for all the stories and insights, and the time she invested in me to study the Proverbs. I invite her from the realms of eternity to continue to lead, guide, and direct each of us in our steps through the pages of this volume.

Finally, to all readers and e-book listeners, whomsoever you might be, Grandma has cautioned me, saying, "Baby, do not tell them everything at once, but remember how I waited on you to read Proverbs for yourself? It was needful and necessary for you to see the words with your own eyes, so Grandma waited for you to study the words of Proverbs to get your own personal insights first; you must need to do this for readers and hearers also."

The sensation from the vibration of those words from Grandma brought a profound and impactful memory into the mind of MrJames. It was as if he was hearing Grandma repeating some things, just as she had done throughout his life. MrJames can see in his hindsight reflection that Grandma considered repetition in the art of living essential to experience a positive outcome from the process.

Therefore, Grandma would always repeat the things she said and encouraged me to repeat my reading and study before she would share her insights, or sometimes before telling me a story or anything else. MrJames believes his grandma understood that knowledge and understanding in the art of living is learned and gained "line upon line, precept upon precept, here a little, and there a little" (Isaiah 28:13; 2 Ne 28:30); and as we liken the insights unto ourselves, and apply the knowledge, understanding, teachings, and instructions in the art of living; our learning will increase.

But, skillful Godly wisdom must need be "looked and searched for" by each reader and hearer of these words, "like a hidden treasure" (Prov 2:1-4), and then from Sovereign God—Our Heavenly Father, Supreme Creator, Master Designer of ALL that exists; "wisdom is given" (Prov 2:6).

MrJames believes this principle is an absolute Godly described method for becoming wiser. Furthermore, he believes it confirms the eternal truth of reaping and sowing; seedtime and harvest, causes and effects. He also believes this principle of learning is based on "an irrevocably decreed law in heaven" that MrJames understands as the laws of decisions and consequences (D&C 130:20-21).

Suddenly, in the construct of reality, some-where behind my eyes and between my ears; and from the sacred eternal realm. Grandma said in an inaudible voice: "My mother: your great-great grandmother Postoria revealed to me; and also committed me, to reveal to you; that individual personal investments of time are the only way for personal revelatory insights and enlightenment to come. Therefore, remember,

remember, remember the F.R.O.G. MrJames; don't forget to express your thanks to Grandma for reminding you to Fully Rely On God to teach readers the skillful Godly wisdom and art of living lessons of life from The Book of Proverbs.

ABOUT THE AUTHOR

Darrell “MrJames” Campbell has been studying the Word of God since age twelve, when he first considered the questions: “Where did I come from? Why am I here, and where do I go after this life? Where did God come from?

MrJames has continually studied the Word of God, Holy Bible, Sacred Scriptures, Book of Mormon, Pearl of Great Price, Doctrine and Covenants, and other inspired sacred writings by Prophets, Apostles, and Teachers. MrJames has a God-given love, devotion, and inclination for spiritual study that has guided him in meditating, pondering, reflecting, fasting, and praying for deeper spiritual insight. Since age twelve, he has repeatedly, oftentimes returned to The Book of Proverbs in his search for skillful Godly wisdom, knowledge, and understanding.

Hundreds of hours of dedicated study has spiritually enlightened his mind with personal revelations of insights, understanding, knowledge, and wisdom related to the art of living according to life’s terms, but living life on God’s terms. Practical application of biblical principles in his life, especially Godly teachings from the writings of Proverbs, has given him real-life experiences, insightful life lessons, and has prepared him to present a unique perspective on the art of living. MrJames believes many of the valuable life lessons learned along the pathway of his life-course, while on his journey through the knuckleheadedness of the wilderness of mortality, he could not have learned in any other way.

As such, one of the basic eternal truths he learned was that some things can only be learned here on Earth, and only through first-hand, or hands-on experience and actual engagement in the activity itself. For example, I have never known anyone to learn to ride a bicycle, ride a skateboard, ride a surfboard, water ski, or learn to roller skate without experiencing falling down a few times; and it may be that you even come away with a few scrapes and scratches, bruises and sprains, and even broken bones.

I remind myself that in any communication, the most important thing above all else is to assert all effort to assure, minimize, reduce, and if possible, eliminate any potential for misunderstanding in the interaction or reaction to the correspondence. Since I might just be talking to myself, while remaining mindful of those suggested instructions; and preparing to construct this literary message from a more in-depth perspective, highlights a need for me to aptly define and identify for myself: "what is generally understood universally, accepted, and considered as challenging life events, issues, trials, situations, and circumstances?"

With that foundation of understanding, I acknowledge there

have been times during my life journey I have personally pondered and considered what is the apparent, the obvious, and/or the noticeable nature of my life challenges, afflictions, failures, adversities, trials, and tests of life? As such, I have come to believe, to properly ascertain and discover life lessons learned from my life challenges requires my realization and willing acknowledgment of a truth stated by self-declared Christian Theologian C.S. Lewis. Wherein he asserted: "life is lived forward," (one moment, hour, day, week, month, year, decade, century, or millennium at a time); "but life is understood backwards" (as we pause to remember, review, reflect, and ponder our past life experiences.

Therefore, for my further clarification, I first asked myself and pondered the questions—what is meant by "life challenges" and what have been some "life challenges for me"? At that point, I engaged in an orderly process of pondering, reflecting, reviewing, and fasting with prayerful consideration many of my personal life experiences, the life experiences of others, life experiences recorded in scriptures, the lives of living Apostles and Prophets, and spiritual principles and teachings of the restored gospel of Jesus Christ.

Generally speaking, talking to myself, I would define a real-life challenging test of life to be a situation and/or a real-life circumstance that brings a clashing collision of my natural human desires, fleshly appetites, feelings, tendencies, emotions, and/or reactions that are in direct opposition to suggested Christian character, Christ-like responses, and morally accepted conduct and behaviors. Specifically, as stated in the Book of Mormon, "The natural man is an enemy to God…unless through the atonement of Christ he puts off the natural man…" (Mosiah 3:19).

Furthermore, the clashing of my natural man impulses and responses to real-life challenging events sometimes manifest in my conduct and behavior as outright rejection or a refusal to obey Christian principles.

However, it may manifest as subtle non-compliance, stiff-necked stubbornness, actual rebellion, specific immoral behavior, disobey commandments, and neglect of eternal principles of the gospel (i.e., tithing, forgiveness, loving others, honor parents, Sabbath day observance, sustaining leaders, etc.).

Since I know I might just be talking to myself, I reflect and consider reactions to my current, personal, and real-time life- challenges, including circumstances that are inherent to the art of living. Pondering situations that are influencing and affecting my life journey in real-time, on a daily basis, and can have eternal consequences.

My responses and choices to life's challenges, the consequences, and the outcomes can be good and positive, thereby pushing me forward toward my eternal created destiny and purpose. On the other hand, my responses and choices can be negative, and therefore hinder, stifle, frustrate, and even stagnate eternal spiritual growth in the direction of the preordained—thought-out beforehand divine destiny. Daily choices can lead us to "prove the good, acceptable and perfect will of God" (Rom 12:1-2); and strengthening our testimony, or they can ultimately be in opposition to Heavenly Father and the "plan of happiness," facilitating immortality, perversion, and negative outcomes in the art of living (Rom 7:14-20; Alma 41:1-10).

As I ponder a hindsight perspective of the art of living canvas of my life journey, it is apparent to me that real-time life challenges—afflictions, trials, and tests—can manifest as solo challenges, or compounded as multiple simultaneous challenges of two or more at a time, as experienced by Job all in a 24hr period. However, in the Bible, 1 John 2:16 and Matthew 4:1-11, it specifically suggests temptations of life spring up in three worldly areas of challenge: (1) lust of the flesh—"command that these stones be made bread"; (2) lust of the eye—Devil offered and "showed to [Jesus] all the kingdoms of the world"; (3) pride of life—doubtfully and with contempt he said to Jesus: "If thou be the Son of God..."

During my six and a half decades of trials and errors, as construction continues on my art of living canvas, and for this conversation with myself, I have further divided, clarified, and attempted to simplify my own understanding of those areas of life challenges:

1—Physical Body—health, fitness, wellness, sickness, disease (fleshly lusts & appetites);

2—Quality of Life—mental, intellectual, IQ, emotional, psychological (autonomy);

3—Financial—haves, have-nots, love money, greed, materialistic (pride);

4—Relationships—Godhead, self, family, marriage, humanity, animals, planet (respect);

5—Agency vanity, disobedience, selfishness, dishonesty, integrity —(choice & accountability);

Since I might just be talking to myself, keeping all aforementioned thoughts and suggestions in mind, I wish to define what I have labeled as the art of living—the determination to keep moving forward no matter what life may throw your way—in the process of time it must need to come to pass in the art of living that we become "willing to submit to all things…" (Mosiah 3:19).

As I concentrate on living forward one day at a time, I am becoming focused on specific life challenges that the Supreme Creator is allowing into my life, for my learning, for my experience, and ultimately intended as a benefit to me in this present existence, "in the presence of mine enemies" (Psalm 23:5), or for a benefit to me at some future time in the eternities. Recording my words in print to deliver this message has single focused my reflecting upon my six and a half decades of life experience and the ongoing construction on my personal art of living canvas. This exercise brings into my mind a consciousness of the footprints I have left behind in the sands of my life journey.

Consequently, I acknowledge in my mind's eye a newly recognized area of weakness and life challenge that I now perceive to be a source of struggle for me in my second estate of existence.

I realized I am currently engaged in, and I am a student of the life challenge I will label as acceptance—a surrender of my will, patiently waiting on the Lord in service to others, learning to be content in my experiences, and resting in the tender mercies of the Lord.

Acceptance is described in scripture as learning to be spiritually "content" (Alma 29:3); being at ease (Phil 4:12-13); to fear not (Heb 13:5-6); being of good cheer (1 Tim 6:6-12); and ultimately learning to perceive challenges in life as "pure joy" (James 1:2-3).

While preparing this message from the depths of my thoughts, and from revealed insights of Grandma, I came to believe spiritual acceptance and spiritual contentment was implied by the Savior in His choice of words: "Take no thought" (Matt. 6:25-27); and alluded to in the words by Paul, who was also Saul, when he said: "Be careful for nothing" and not unduly concerned or anxious about anything (Philippians 4:6-7). Similarly, my brother Karl—Short Coat believes what Solomon instructed and taught: "Do not boast, [brag or worry] about tomorrow; no one knows what the next day will bring"(Prov 26:1)

MrJames believes it is significant in the art of living that we all must need come to accept the proverbial truth that "life is, what it is" in the current moment; undoubtedly, even in this period of economic uncertainty and this post-pandemic moment of living in these latter-days. Therefore, as God's servant Job would probably affirm, and as Grandma might say: "Baby, we ought to be thankful to God things are as well as they are because Job would surely tell you that things can always be worse than they are. After having done the best we can and ALL we can do; and it truly is ALL we can do, the art of living demands that we must allow contentment and acceptance to permeate and surround the situations and circumstances of our life."

ACCEPTANCE

"...acceptance is the answer to all my problems today."

When I am disturbed, it is because I find some person, place, or situation - some fact of my life - unacceptable to me, and I can find no serenity (no peace) until I accept that person, place, thing, or situation as being exactly the way it is supposed to be [in that] moment.

Nothing, absolutely nothing, happens in God's world by mistake, [accident, chance, luck, or just coincidence]. "We may throw the dice....but God determines how they fall" (Prov 16:33).

Until I [can accept my life challenges as being tailor-made for my eternal benefit and]... [learn to] accept life on [God's omnipotent, omniscient, and omnipresent] terms, [and truly doing all I can to be the best "me" that I can], I cannot be happy.

[Therefore], I need to concentrate not so much on what needs to be changed in the world and others, and more on what needs to be changed in me, and in my attitudes." Accept[ing] the things I cannot change and [taking steps with] courage, to change the things I can; [applying Godly] wisdom [and discernment] to know the difference.

And I just might be talking to myself.

Adopted by MrJames LifeCoach from: "AA Big Book" 449 Third Edition ~~ "AA Big Book" Page 417 Fourth Edition.

PRELUDE

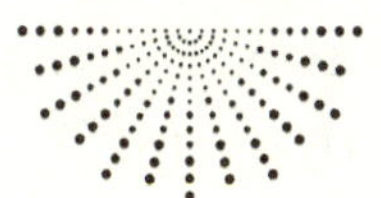

MrJames, finding himself unable to see himself as a child of God, feeling separated from God and all alone, struggling with substance abuse and destructive addictive behaviors, entangled with serious family discord, and carrying other unspoken burdens, his thoughts turned back to heaven.

MrJames began to reflect upon the words of one of his mother's favorite scriptures: "Your help cometh from the Lord" (Psalms 121:1-2). The lonely road he had to travel to recover from his separation from God was a pathway less traveled, and the process to achieve success was even lesser understood.

MrJames believes his journey may have blazed a trail and taught him some valuable, useful, and practical lessons in the art of living. MrJames realizes and further acknowledges that he could not have learned many of the valuable lessons he learned in any other way.

Suddenly, riding in on the sound of a whisper, MrJames can perceive a still soft voice seemingly coming forth into the construct of his present reality, but firmly rooted in an experience from the past. Nonetheless, within that flash of insight, he recalls his son Darrell Jr learning to ride a skateboard, from more than thirty years ago. Recalling that Jr Frog had grabbed hold on the side of my car one day, as I was coasting down the street.

Suddenly, we hit a rough spot in the road; I heard a thump, then a scream. Consequently, a visit to the emergency room revealed, Jr had sustained a broken wrist. As such, in the art of living, just as in learning to ride and enjoying to ride a skateboard, oftentimes there are slips, stumbles, trips, and falls.

The most fundamental truth MrJames learned from an assortment of experiences was: God absolutely controls all things, not just the good things of life, literally all things of life, both heavenly and earthly. Furthermore, MrJames believes there is no such thing as a true accident; as such, nothing happens in this world by mistake—unforeseen by the creator and unintended or unpermitted.

The Bible teaches that, "all things work together for good to them that love God, to them who are the called according to his purpose" (Romans 8:28). Be attentive and consciously mindful that the Bible did not say all good things, but it is written "all things." The author believes this means things we consider undesirable, adversarial, bad, and even unpleasant things as well as "good" things; all work together for our (Christians) intended good. MrJames learned this essential truth while entangled in addictive behaviors leaving him feeling powerless and out of control.

How do you gain unyielding confidence that God can bring peace in times of trouble? Faith comes by hearing and hearing by the word of God. More importantly, skillful Godly wisdom comes from exposure, from reading, and from time invested in the study of the Word of God. As stated in the first five chapters of Proverbs: one purpose of The Book of Proverbs is to make the "simple, ... the fool, and the... foolish" wise; wiser, and prudent.

This sure confidence (faith) in The Book of Proverbs and the Word of God, the author gained traveling through tragedy, chaos, confusion, times of disappointment, uncertainty, and abandonment.

Consequently, over five years of consistent daily study of a chapter of Proverbs each day, from personal incidents and experiences the author has learned how to embrace an unexplainable state of inner peace in tumultuous times of testings, uncertainty, trials, and tribulation.

FOREWORD

Angel Seise

I'm only just midway in my reading, and already I am motivated to record and register this quotable comment:

In his first book, "Death to F.R.O.G.S.: The Art of Living," MrJames LifeCoach takes you through a biographical journey as a former addict in an allegorical style, in and out of the present time to flashbacks of memorable life-lessons, anecdotal experiences, paradigm shifts, and rude awakenings. I heartily recommend this thought-provoking, insightful, and motivational book.

Minister Angel Seise Light of Joy Church Men of Valor Riverdale, Georgia.

Bonnie Cephus

As a long-time associate and Sister in Christ of the author, I was given the honor of being one of the first to read the aforementioned book.

As such, I would like to offer interested persons the following synopsis: "Death To F.R.O.G.S.: The Art of Living" is a poignant story of a young boy raised up in the Deep South by his grandmother who became his legally adopted mother. As the story unfolds, we learn of the parables and lessons the grandmother taught him, and how these stories became stepping stones for change in the latter part of the young man's life. The author takes us on a journey through the tumultuous early years of his growing up in the Jim Crow era of the Deep South, where he had to learn to navigate racism and the desegregation of the public school where he attended in his hometown of Prichard, just on the outskirts of Mobile, Alabama, at the height of the Civil Rights Movement in the late 1960s through the 1970s.

MrJames LifeCoach tells the story in the second person, in a colorful and anecdotal manner that is intriguing and exciting. And it is in the 3rd and 4th chapters where you will begin to understand that "Death To F.R.O.G.S.: The Art of Living" is much more than the story of a young man who grew up in a Christian family and a loving community and who was guided by the deep love and lessons taught and lived by Grandma. The author chronicles his life into adulthood where he had to navigate through the trauma of his alcoholic stepfather's murder of his birth mother, the rearing of younger siblings, fatherhood, and marriage at the tender age of eighteen (18) years old. The author lends insights of his success as a student of higher education, his many academic and civic accolades that culminated in his being a successful Restaurant Owner and CEO. Only to find himself, in later years, losing his business, in financial ruin; and motivated by the pain, shame, and feelings of worthlessness he searches and finds what he terms as a "counterfeit feel-good sensation."

Thus, in spite of his Christian upbringing, a loving family, education, and success as an entrepreneur, the author finds himself in the fight of his life. He becomes chemically dependent, and the struggle to overcome destructive addictive behaviors forces him to reach deep inside himself to develop the knowledge and skills to triumph over these negative life forces, that he now calls the Frogs of life. Going forward, in describing the overcoming of these forces, he called the process "Death To F.R.O.G.S.: The Art of Living."

Get ready to be taken on another mind-blowing journey; as our author gives us lessons and principles in: "Art of Living: Lessons From Proverbs—Remember F.R.O.G." as well as insights on absolute truths that are useful in the art of living and for alleviating the "frogs" from our lives.

From the author's expansive six decades of insights, and his delving into literature, science, psychology, philosophy, religion, and spirituality; and after having read "Death To F.R.O.G.S.," the reader is bound to come away from this book motivated with renewed excitement and conviction of how they can F-ully R-ely O-n G-od to improve in the art of living in the divinely created purpose of their own lives, applying, and simply using the daily routine of F.R.O.G. principles and the skillful Godly wisdom set forth in this book: "Art of Living: Lessons From Proverbs—Remember F.R.O.G."

Bonnie; Cephus MS Psychology Clinical Psychologist Union Springs, Alabama

As the author, MrJames completes reading the reviews from Angel and Bonnie of his book: "Death To F.R.O.G.S.: The Art of Living," and as he prepares to move forward in unfolding the story behind book two: "The Art of Living: Lessons From Proverbs—Remember F.R.O.G.," he begins to feel a profound sense of influence from the eternal realms. Suddenly, in his conscious awareness, there is Grandma, Grandfather Richard, and TEACHER. They were all present; and in an inaudible synchronized and unified voice, he heard these words: "Baby, we came to alert and warn you and readers about this book—Art of Living: Lessons From Proverbs—Remember F.R.O.G."

Feeling intrigued, perplexed, and cautious; MrJames was thinking to himself: what is the warning about? In the same unified voice, the answer came: "In the art of living in a manner to produce the more positive outcomes in life, there must need be an exchange of spiritual insights from eternal realms revealed into present physical reality. However, the Prince of the Air—enemy of mankind will attempt to blind the eyes and close the ears of readers to the insights that are concealed and which can only be revealed to those who voluntarily choose to accept the challenge and become a reader of Book of Proverbs—aka Book of Wisdom." MrJames wanted to know what he must need to do next, but before he could ask the question his answer came through: "MrJames, in this book: Art of Living: Lessons From Proverbs—Remember F.R.O.G., you must need to issue a challenge for readers to make a commitment to themselves to read a Chapter-A-Day from Proverbs. Write the story that we will direct from the eternal realms, and the story will unlock the skillful Godly wisdom of the Proverbs, insights, and understanding that will be revealed behind the eyes and in between the ears of the committed readers and all those who answer the challenge."

MrJames wanted to know more but was only told: "Remember F.R.O.G. and tell readers they must need to voluntarily keep the main thing the main thing; pray first, aim high, and stay focused; because the adversary of life and of the art of living, he is on the prowl. And, just like a roaring lion, he is seeking whomsoever he may devour, delay, frighten, scare, and detour away from their created life purpose." MrJames noticed in his conscious awareness that the presence of his visitors from the eternal realms was fading into the distance and becoming just vaguely detectable. The final words understood by MrJames was: "MrJames, we must say no more; but you must write the stories of your insights from six decades in the art of living; from your personal exposure to the Skillful Godly Wisdom; and from the insights gained from five years of your daily reading a chapter from Proverbs. We still do not tell you it all, more is yet to be but will be yet revealed; and you must need to not tell readers everything." MrJames remembers being told that divine guiding principles of life are concealed in the Proverbs for all readers to find; and in the eternal realms they have ALL prayed: "may the readers find them as they answer the challenge of: Art of Living: Lessons from Proverbs—Remember F.R.O.G. and gain insights from the stories MrJames will use to deliver this message..." Then there was silence.....

INTRODUCTION

In my efforts of striving for wisdom, knowledge, understanding, and seeking Godly wisdom, since I was twelve years old, I have immersed myself in the study of the Word of God. At that age, my grandmother was the most influential adult role model figure in my life. My Grandma was born in 1902; she was the offspring of Black Creek Indians of Central Alabama; she was soft-spoken, compassionate, friendly, and focused on being the best person she could be. In my formative years, she became the standard that I have used throughout my life to recognize, comprehend, and understand Godly love, compassion, commitment, devotion, and integrity.

Grandma Willie Inez Campbell (aka "Ma'dear"), when I was around 7 years old, at the death of my grandfather Richard Norris Campbell, became my living, guiding art of living blueprint, and my example of devotion to family.

Grandma believed in God, Jesus, the Spirit; regularly we attended Baptist Churches, and she taught us to pray. She had several favorite Bible verses she often repeated, but I soon noticed she would repeat one of the verses or one of her unique sayings only when she believed her words would bring clarity to some situation or circumstance that she felt made the verse applicable. In retrospect, as I look back, in the art of living, I believed she was the wisest person of my childhood days. However, at age 14, it was amazing and remarkable to me to learn, after her death, that she only had a formal 3rd Grade education.

Ma'Dear had great delight in having the Bible read to her because she could not read or write very well. She would radiate pure joy in her facial expressions whenever someone was reading to her from the Bible, especially when they were reading one of her favorite chapters. Sometimes she would put out her hand as if to say stop; then she would say, "Hold up, slow down just a minute, you got a fire to go put out or something?" Then she would start to recite from memory as many of the verses that she had memorized. She would say with a smile on her face, "My momma and my grandma told me that story over and over again, and I never forgot."

I now realize that as I was sitting there listening to Grandma recite her stories, she would add her insights and impressions meant to make the point of the story easier to understand. I know my grandma was transferring wisdom, knowledge, understanding, and valuable art of living spiritual insights to me. My grandmother had three favorite things she cherished from the time investment her parents and grandparents (my great-great-grandparents) made in her as they would spend time sharing their biblical knowledge and spiritual understanding with her.

I believe the first thing you need to know about my grandma is that she thought the most important book on Earth was the Bible, and the most important book to read in the Bible was Proverbs—also known by them as the book of skillful Godly wisdom. My grandmother rarely raised her voice much above a whisper, as I can remember, but she would increase the tone in her voice and sternly say, "How could anyone give another person good Godly advice, on anything that really mattered in the art of living, unless the person giving the advice, at the very least, had been exposed to that book of Godly wisdom?"

I know it was my grandma and her art of living life that inspired me, by the time I was 12 years old, to begin reading the Bible for myself. At 12 years old, the first book of the Bible I read all the way through, including all 31 chapters, was The Book of Proverbs. I have often wondered why that was the first full book of chapters I would read. I feel the presence of my grandma, and as I see her on the screen of my mind, she is sitting at my feet waiting to hear from me. She wants to hear the Godly wisdom, knowledge, understanding, and insights that I have gleaned, received, retained, and applied to my life.

It is with exceedingly great joy that I express gratitude to Grandma for exposing me to The Book of Wisdom. Another thing about Grandma, I feel I should share, as I can hear the whispering of her voice inside me; behind my eyes, and between my ears. I hear my Grandma saying to me, something she often repeated to me when I was struggling with F.R.O.G.S. of life, real-life challenges, and life-controlling difficulties in the art of living. Grandma would say: "Baby, come closer"; in a soft whisper whenever she was about to share art of living insights from her life, with someone she cares about and wants her life lessons to be helpful to them. It is my intention in this volume, to introduce readers to her voice: "Baby come closer, so I can tell you something."

Meet Grandma

In this volume, MrJames shares a perspective he was taught by his grandma. She would say: "You are a precious child of the Most High, All Mighty, and All Powerful God. So, when you find yourself troubled with f.r.o.g.s. of life, and it seems you are unable to overcome that challenge in your life; especially if you have been dealing with the matter repeatedly and unsuccessfully for a long time; Baby, then it could mean that there is something about the situation; the circumstance; or the f.r.o.g.s. you have been unable to rid from your life, that you just simply don't understand."

One day speaking from this perspective, MrJames remembers his grandma saying: "Baby, my momma read to me from the Bible where it said: God's people are destroyed because of a lack of understanding" and MrJames also believes it is because they have either refused or rejected the Word of God; they have never been exposed to the Word of God, and are ignorant to what God has said. That was the day she asked me: "Baby, do you not know you are one of God's people?"

Therefore, for readers and listeners, MrJames has prepared this volume just in case you may need to invest some time in yourself to study The Book of Wisdom and find out what God has said about the art of living and the f.r.o.g.s in your life. MrJames encourages each reader and listener with words his grandma always ended their conversations with: "I hope you find this is helpful Baby, now you go and talk to

God and see what HE has to say about words of advice I have shared with you."

Grandma believed these two things are true: first, that there was not a right way to do a wrong thing; and if you pray and ask God he will answer. So she would always insist that the person receiving her advice, always prayed to ask God if her advice was right, truthful, and wise. Grandma told me many times when there was a need for me to make a decision about doing or not doing something; I was unsure about the best way to do that something; I wanted to do it and even felt strongly that the thing needed to be done.

Continuing to talk to himself and pondering through the many times young MrJames came to Grandma with such dilemmas, her response is engraved between his ears and behind his eyes such that, it is as if he can hear the whisper of her voice saying: "Baby, it surely seems to be a simple answer to that thing in my simple mind. You got the cart before the horse."

She would always pause, and then continue in her still, soft voice: "Baby, the main thing for you to do is to keep the main thing the main thing, and keep first things first. Pray to God to find out if what you want, or what you want to do, is right or wrong (D&C 9:7-8). If it is the right thing to do, then you can ask God for the right way, to do that thing. However, if what you want to do is wrong; then the problem is that there is not a right way to do a wrong thing Baby."

As I continue to introduce my grandma throughout this volume, I prepare readers and listeners to receive impressions, and feelings, and insights from my six decades of consistent exposure to skillful Godly wisdom from Proverbs; and her inspiring influence on my life in the construct of my art of living.

For over five years, MrJames have consistently read each day from The Book of Proverbs, each day reading the chapter that corresponded with the date of the month. The second life-guiding belief of Grandma is now flashing on the screen of his mind like a neon sign. MrJames can perceive her still soft voice, behind his eyes and from between my ears; he is reminded of her most repeated Biblical verse.

MrJames realizes Grandma will be aware and attentive, even from the eternal realms, as he talks to himself and shares insights with readers and listeners; primarily because of the importance of the messages in this volume.

MrJames remembers Grandma had memorized her #1 favorite Bible verse that was found in the Book of James: "If anyone lacked wisdom (like me, she would say), let them ask of God, who gives wisdom to the simple-minded (like me, she would say), and HE will give it to them generously" (James 1:5-8). In his life, Grandma was like a diamond in the rough, his personal tutor; and he was raised feeling like he was an apprentice to both his grandparents in the art of living. MrJames revered Grandma as his proverbial "ace in the hole" and to him she was like a sleeping giant, his best-kept secret, and his most cherished possession. Grandma often surprised Young MrJames with her authentic, and original thoughts on spiritual matters. Such as the insights she shared with him on her #1 favorite book of all the 66 books of the Bible.

Grandma reminded him that the Apostle James was the half-brother of Jesus; and the words in the Book of James were a written letter from him to believers and non-believers, and even to his Jewish crucifiers. Grandma explained to him that she always felt James writes compassionately from a deep, close, intimate perspective and testimony of Jesus and he had been taught by his older half- brother. MrJames came to believe that the letter written by Apostle James dissects and analyzes faith, patience, and love. He learned from Grandma, and came to know those three as the powerful "spiritual triplets" in the art of living.

Grandma believed Apostle James wants the readers of his letter to know some things from their brother-to-brother upbringing and perspective, that began long before HE—his half-brother was introduced to the world, and before HE was found in the temple teaching when he was 12 years old. As siblings and teenagers growing up together in the same house; Grandma had imagined and intuitively realized these brothers probably laid in their beds after the candles went out, or were put out, and they likely had some private conversations; personal, brother-to-brother bonding time, just as any other brothers would have had.

Grandma imagined, and persuaded MrJames to believe, that there was a greater potential for them to do so because one of the brothers was Jesus. Grandma often reminded MrJames that she felt it is from experiences and foundations of that intimate relationship that James is writing; and his letter is meant to teach and testify to both the believing saints, and all the Nations of the Earth. Grandma believed and shares her Godly wisdom and insights into those private conversations with MrJames along with his reading and study of Proverbs.

He remembers Grandma was sure those conversations were not recorded anywhere known, except for being etched in memory by James, and no doubt influenced his letter.

Furthermore, it is an accepted fact the letter was not written until AD 40-50; as James was inspired after the days of Jesus. Grandma could not have known that biblical scholars believed her favorite book of James; could be among the first written books of the New Testament. Knowing this, MrJames can hear her still, soft, whispering voice say to readers and listeners: "Baby, come closer so you can hear from MrJames; and then read and re-read the letter from the Apostle James. Care to read it slow with a desire to understand the deeper messages from the mind of James; and receive insights from me from the eternal realms, and in words on these pages of perceptions on Proverbs, from MrJames."

Grandma believed that readers with a desire to know, seeking with real intent, and with a Godly purpose may find that Apostle James could have placed hidden nuggets of insights of insights, that James only understood when he took time to look back in hindsight, after Jesus Christ—Teacher—his half-brother was no longer alive in the flesh.

In the personal experiences of MrJames, being encouraged and prompted by his grandma, he found that after his fifth time of reading this complete book, and after the fifth complete reading of any sacred Scriptures; MrJames

testifies to readers that there will be divine revelations of insights, skillful Godly wisdom and understanding that will flow down upon the reader. MrJames believes, as it was suggested by Grandma, that there is revelatory spiritual significance to the book written by Apostle James.

Grandma testified of this to me, in the whisper of her still, soft voice, as I am recording these words. It is as if I can hear her saying to me, "Baby, come closer," and then, to my surprise, in a more pronounced voice, I feel the vibrations of her voice deep in the recesses of my inner being. She is saying, "Baby, tell the readers to make a time investment in themselves each day; ask them to read a chapter from The Book of Proverbs each day that corresponds to the date of the month; let them know the secret I shared with you when you were 12 years old; about The Book of Wisdom.

MrJames remembers the message from his mother's mother, Willie Inez Campbell; his great-great grandmother, Postoria Mosley; when he was 12 years old. She told him from a dying bed that it was her who taught Grandma about the existence of a spiritual connection between The Book of Proverbs, the Book of James, and the art of living the foreordained—divine, destined, and thought-out beforehand purpose of your life (Jeremiah 29:11).

MrJames remembers, on that day, he and Grandma perceived that message behind their eyes and between their ears at the same time. That was the day MrJames started to read The Book of Proverbs; and he also recalls that great grandma Bernice Alls, and great grandma Postoria Mosley both came to him in a dream.

Somehow, from the realms of eternity, Grandma was there in his dream; and her presence made the dream seem like reality. Simultaneously, but in an inaudible voice, they asked MrJames to share with readers all stories that they had taught to Grandma, and all the stories Grandma had taught me.

As the essence of their presence, and the presence of Grandma began to fade and wane away, they said, "Baby, as you are sharing, and as you continue to share all the stories, you are being prepared; and you will be preparing others in the art of living. Repeatedly reading the Proverbs, seeking for divine insights, hearing and hearing (Rom 10:17) the words and the stories will shed light on the pathway for others to follow that leads to the discovery of their divinely created life purpose."

MrJames was ushered back into present reality, but behind his eyes and between his ears, his perspective of reality and imagination was being transformed.

MrJames was physically drained and his strength was nearly

depleted, but he remembered in the dream Grandma had also revealed something to him in an inaudible manner. She informed him about the dream she had the night of her birthday party, the night before the day when she had died. Grandma informed MrJames in that dream that she was pleased with him in the art of living; and that he had been sufficiently prepared for his preordained life purpose.

Then, somewhat hurriedly but not abruptly, Grandma began to make her presence known to MrJames. Inaudibly she said to MrJames, "When you saw me in your dream with the other grandmothers, each of them asked me if I had consistently repeated the stories to you? And they asked me if I had repeated and recited from memory my favorite Bible verses that had been etched into my mind, and written on the tablet of my inner self?"

Suddenly, but in a graceful reverent tone, as if she could read my mind; Grandma said, "You do not recall the promise they gave you in your dream, do you?" MrJames answered and said no, he did not.

Then, feeling as if she had a wide smile on her face, and was ready to give him a warm and fuzzy embrace, Grandma said: "Your love, your delight, your burning desire, the Insights, and the revelatory understanding that came to you as you would consistently read and study The Book of Proverbs; and as you took pleasure in learning to apply the principles of God's holy word in the art of living; Baby, it is time for you to know those were gifts bestowed on you from the heavenly realms; and All are divine gifts that were given to assist you in filling the full measure of your created purpose; and when your time had fully come, I was to share my eternal insights; and the Word of God deposited in me through those shared stories."

Grandma assured MrJames that the time he had chosen to invest in the art of living, reading, and studying of the Word of God, consistently doing so, until the Word was deep inside of him, and consequently MrJames would be armed and protected from the enemy of life; who is in all ways against, and in opposition to all that is righteous, good, and acceptable, and fights against the perfect will of the Most High God—Our Heavenly Father—Supreme Creator—and Master Designer of all that exists.

Grandma sounded perfectly pleased and pleasant as she continued in her inaudible still, small, soft voice, and MrJames intuitively knew this was a "Baby come closer" moment. In his mind's eye, it was as if MrJames could see she was leaning forward.

Then Grandma whispered, seemingly from between his ears and from behind his eyes, saying to him: "Your time has come, you are ready. Just remember the F.R.O.G. and go tell the readers and the listeners that whoever would invest the time to read and re-read The Book of Proverbs, they are promised to begin receiving revelatory insight, Godly wisdom, increased understanding, and divine instructions in the art of living."

The promise received in the depths of MrJames and Grandma's soul that day was assurance that divine favor and choice blessings would be showered down upon the diligent readers of Proverbs. The readers and hearers who stayed exposed to and engaged in reading and studying the Word of God, and consistently gleaning insights to apply to the art of living, would be abundantly blessed.

As the presence of Grandma and other ancestors was beginning to gradually fade and wane away, Grandma reminded MrJames that our ancestors prayed on behalf of the readers and hearers, praying to "The Most High God—Our Heavenly Father—Supreme Creator—Master Designer of All that exists" and saying: "Father, may the BLOOD of Jesus—the Lamb of God, the spirit of wisdom, the spirit of knowledge, the spirit of understanding, and divine protection surround MrJames and all of you. I say no more now.

In the name of Jesus Christ. Amen.

1

DAY 1 - INVITATION: SEEK GODLY WISDOM

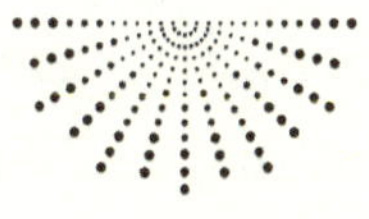

PROVERBS 1

Hello friends, readers, and hearers. Today is the first day of the month. Having been persuaded, urged, enticed, and beckoned by Grandma, MrJames LifeCoach requests, asks, suggests, pleads, encourages, beseeches, challenges, and strongly desires you to join him each day in reading through The Book of Proverbs.

For nearly five years, being influenced and guided from the eternal realms, MrJames LifeCoach has been on a journey and quest of relentlessly striving to read the chapter from The Book of Proverbs each day that also corresponds with the date of the month. Today, because it is the first day of the month, he continues with chapter one.

MrJames LifeCoach invites whomsoever that will, to join with him in his daily perusals through the writings of Proverbs. Under the oversight of Grandma, he reads and sometimes shares insights and reflections gained from his ongoing daily exposure and study of Proverbs. His preferred translation is the King James Version; however, these shared insights are compiled by him from his study of the New King James, the New Living Translation, the New International Version, and the Amplified Classic Version of the Holy Bible.

Primarily, first and foremost, Grandma always reminded MrJames to keep in mind that one of the intended purposes, as stated in the initial chapters of The Book of Proverbs, is to expose the readers not just to wisdom (Prov 1:2), but to expose and introduce "skillful Godly wisdom" (Prov 1:1- 7) that comes from God—The Most High God—Our Heavenly Father—Supreme Creator, and Master Designer of all that exists.

Apparent to MrJames, and suggested by Grandma, it was the teachings contained within Proverbs and also practiced by Solomon that caused him to become the richest and wisest person to have lived on Earth.

<u>A thought from MrJames LifeCoach on Proverbs 1:</u>

Since I might just be talking to myself, I know within my inner self that my nearly fifty years of on and off; and on and off again of reading, studying, and applying the wisdom of Proverbs has had incalculable positive and profound effects in my life. Primarily, supplying readers with divine tools for the art of living that will produce positive outcomes is the inherent and built-in purpose of The Book of Proverbs; a.k.a. The Book of Wisdom.

However, as I unhurriedly read through this chapter with in-depth pondering, reflecting, focused on, and thinking about the art of living, I gained a benefit in the art of living from this hindsight introspection.

Furthermore, remaining fixated on my more than six decades of real-life experiences, I surmise and conclude that I am getting "too soon Old, and too late Smart."

Nevertheless, it is attributed to my unrelenting study of The Book of Proverbs that I came to recognize, I am gradually becoming a bit wiser. Moreover, even amongst my "knuckleheaded" failures, amid inconsistency in the application of principles taught in Proverbs, my efforts of persisting and continuing to read chapters from the words of Proverbs were not in vain (Isaiah 55:11).

Moreover, I testify to the truth that my efforts ongoing exposure, and study of Proverbs was contributing to transforming my art of living life outcomes, life perspectives, and my real-life worldview. More importantly, persistent practical application of the principles seems to facilitate order in my life priorities, and make clear the guidelines in the art of living.

Furthermore, I do not see myself as I have in the past, just a reflection of a self-described: "A #1 Knucklehead." I am increasingly more accepting, consciously more aware, and willingly more prompt to admit that all past life experiences are exceedingly valuable and priceless to me in the art of living. Each experience, episode, and chapter of life experience has contributed a benefit to me. Influenced by Grandma and study of Proverbs, MrJames LifeCoach set sail on a divine journey to become a reflection of a person motivated by skillful Godly wisdom in the art of living, and filled with inspired desire to fill the full measure of their created purpose.

Keeping all the aforementioned words and thoughts from Grandma and MrJames LifeCoach, in mind, and internalizing the skillful and godly wisdom of Chapter One; let us read, study, and share thoughts as we each willingly choose to observe, apply in practical ways, and take upon ourselves "skillful Godly wisdom" by daily reading from The Book of Wisdom—a.k.a. The Book of Proverbs.

Remember: He who knows and knows he knows is wise. However, he who knows but knows not that he knows is yet still unlearned, immature, and ignorant.

In the name of Jesus Christ. Amen.

2

DAY 2 - INVITATION: HEED CORRECTION

PROVERBS 2

Hello new friends, readers, and hearers. Today is the second day of the month. MrJames LifeCoach requests, asks, suggests, pleads, encourages, beseeches, challenges, and strongly desires for you to join him each day in his reading through The Book of Proverbs.

MrJames LifeCoach invites whomsoever that will, to join with him each day as he reads, shares, and sometimes posts his insights and reflections from his daily perusals through the writings of Proverbs. Grandma has reminded MrJames to let readers and hearers know his preferred translation is the King James Version; however, his shared insights are compiled and incorporated from his study of the New King James; the New Living Translation; the New International Version; and the Amplified Classic Version of the Holy Bible.

Consequently, MrJames reminds readers and hearers that another one of the intended purposes of The Book of Proverbs is to expose readers not just to wisdom, but to expose them to "skillful and godly" discernment, respect, and reverence for God; and spiritual knowledge with understanding (Prov 2: 1-5).

Whomsoever will incline their ears to treasure, observe, and apply the instructions of Proverbs will receive divine guidance and protection from the enemy of life, and from the pitfalls in the pathway to mastering the "art of living" journey (Prov 2: 1-5).

Reading this chapter of Proverbs, MrJames can hear the whisper of Grandma saying: "Sound wisdom comes from The Most High God—Heavenly Father, The Supreme Creator, and Master Designer of all that exists (Prov 2: 6-8). MrJames reminds readers again that it was the teachings contained within Proverbs that were learned, experienced, taught, and practiced by Solomon that lead him to become the rich and wisest person to have lived on earth.

A thought from MrJames LifeCoach on Proverbs 2:

MrJames LifeCoach acknowledges that there seems to be an unwritten theme surfacing and permeating throughout this chapter. Seemingly, the rising theme and premise imply, giving the impression, and suggesting in no uncertain terms that the pathway that leads to peace and serenity is conditional. In other words, inherent to the accomplishment of our divinely created purpose is predicated upon, associated with, connected to, and aligned with our personal authenticity—honesty and integrity, discretion—good judgment, and righteousness—being in right standing with The Most High God—Our Heavenly Father—Supreme Creator—Master Designer of all that exists.

Moreover, the presence of this theme and premise is reflected, not only in the beginning chapters of Proverbs but saturated and taught throughout the entire collection of Proverbs.

Therefore, it follows that recognizing, understanding, accepting, and connecting the significance of this principle is a foundational prerequisite; and a pre-requirement in the art of living according to our higher and divinely created purpose. MrJames LifeCoach submits to new friends, readers, and hearers that you should also recognize the prevalent and repetitious, intentional, and deliberate early placement of this theme and premise by Solomon.

Notably, moving forward in the art of living our higher callings; and to reap our greatest eternal benefits we are instructed to avoid the seductress woman, to avoid perverseness in our deeds and speech, and in our interactions with others. Furthermore, from repeated study of The Book of Wisdom, MrJames has ascertained and discovered that maintaining our integrity is addressed all throughout The Book of Proverbs. However, directly and specifically it is referenced and expounded upon vividly in this chapter (Prov 2: 22).

Remember, do not procrastinate and delay, "Now is the time for readers and hearers to prepare to meet God" (Alma 34:32); because he (she) who knows and knows he (she) knows is wise.

However, he (she) who knows but knows not that he (she) knows is yet still unlearned, immature, and ignorant.

In the name of Jesus Christ. Amen.

3

DAY 3 - INVITATION: LIVE THE INSIGHTS

PROVERBS 3

Hello new friends, readers, and hearers. Today is day three since MrJames LifeCoach challenged and announced his strong desire for an audience of readers to join with him each day in reading through The Book of Proverbs. For over five years, MrJames LifeCoach has been reading one chapter each day from Proverbs, reading each day the specific chapter that coincides with that same day of the month.

Today is the third day; if you are taking his challenge for the first time, continue with the reading of chapter 3. MrJames LifeCoach requests whomever will, to join with him today as he compiles his insights from his daily perusals through the writings of Proverbs.

Moreover, he invites you to share with a friend your feedback, insights, and comments. MrJames' preferred translation is the King James Version; however, these shared insights are compiled only as a thumbnail summary from his study of the New King James, the New Living Translation, the New International Version, and the Amplified Classic Version of the Holy Bible. Grandma would have you know that one purpose of The Book of Proverbs is to expose readers to "skillful and godly" wisdom that comes from the Most High God—Heavenly Father, Supreme Creator, Master Designer of all that exists. The teachings of Proverbs were given by God and were practiced by Solomon for the benefit of leading God's people. His following after and obedience to Godly wisdom caused him to become the richest, wisest, and for a time one of the most revered persons to have lived on earth. These shared reflections, insights, and perspectives from MrJames LifeCoach, on each chapter in The Book of Proverbs, were also influenced by the living example of Grandma; they have come from his nearly fifty years of on and off reading, study, and application of the guidance from Proverbs in his life.

MrJames is anxious to testify to readers and hearers that effects in his life and in the art of living have been positive spiritual growth and skillful Godly enlightenment. His challenge to new friends, and to whomever the readers and hearers may be, is to become a student of The Book of Proverbs, learn the principles, apply the teachings, and you will gain evidence-based confirmation of eternal truths.

MrJames LifeCoach has recognized a central theme laced throughout all of Proverbs that is intended to lay out before readers proven ways, if observed, that will effectively lead readers into becoming better at the "Art of Living." Therefore, he guides readers from his perspective as a Certified LifeCoach, in their quest of becoming proficient in the art of living, he adamantly, sternly, and stubbornly encourages you to read The Book of Proverbs. MrJames believes the evidence confirms Proverbs is the ultimate instruction manual in the art of living, and a GPS guide for readers, leading to the better way to live as we create our unique tapestry that reflects our life journey.

Grandma was persistent in her instructions to Young MrJames, that it was his continuous reading, studying, and actual application of the principles taught within Proverbs that was raising consciousness and vibrations within him, and transforming his life perspective, worldview, and aligning his life priorities with his divinely created life purpose. Thus, tutored and mentored by Grandma, internally MrJames was becoming a person with a compelling desire to fill the full measure of his created purpose, whomever you new readers, and three-day readers may be, let us read, study, and share thoughts with friends and family as we gather unto ourselves skillful godly wisdom from Proverbs as we learn to observe and cleave unto skillful Godly wisdom. In so doing, we are calling unto ourselves from the eternal realms a multiplicity of advantages and provisions preordained to help us in the art of living.

A thought from MrJames LifeCoach on Proverbs 3:

It is apparent to me, within this 3rd chapter of Proverbs, there seems to be a reminder to the reader to seek after skillful and godly wisdom. Comparing and declaring Godly wisdom to be "more precious and more to be desired than rubies, gold, or silver" (Prov 3:14-15).

Furthermore, the language of this chapter, again by using no uncertain terms, suggests, asserts, and assures the reader that seeking after and obtaining skillful Godly wisdom can also bring possession of riches, honor, prudence—sound judgment, and can be accompanied and paired with the blessing of lengthening of days.

Additionally, the enlightenment and eternal principles put forth in this chapter remind readers and hearers that as we heed, observe, and obey these guidelines of instructions, with practical application in "all our ways" and "lean not to our own understanding" (Prov 3:5), conducting ourselves accordingly, The Most High God—Our Heavenly Father—Supreme Creator—Master Designer of all that exists will "direct our path."

Therefore, God will position us; place us on that pathway that will lead us to become what we were in fact created to become. As such, we will be in partnership with our Creator and aligning ourselves to accomplish and fulfill our divinely created purpose.

Remember, remember, and remember; this is the day to prepare (Alma 34:32), get prepared, and be prepared; this is

the day to be wise, get wisdom, and become wiser.

4

DAY 4 - INVITATION: SEEK TO KNOW GOD

PROVERBS 4

Hello, another day has arrived, new friends, readers, and hearers. Today is day four for some of you since MrJames LifeCoach requested, challenged, and announced his strong desire for an audience to join with him each day and read through The Book of Proverbs; to gain, review, share, and reflect upon insights and impressions together (www.patreon.com/hardknocks).

As it is, MrJames LifeCoach has been reading through The Book of Proverbs for more than five years; reading the entire chapter from Proverbs each day that coincides with that specific date of the month.

MrJames LifeCoach preferred translation to read is the King James Version; however, these shared insights are compiled by him from his study of the New King James, the New Living Translation, the New International Version, and thc

Amplified Classic Version of the Holy Bible, also. Today is the 4th, therefore he continues with reading chapter 4 with readers and hearers. Whomsoever; friend, friends of friends, strangers, Angels of Light; readers and hearers, join with MrJames LifeCoach as he reflects on his insights, impressions, and personal experiences from his daily perusals through the written words of in The Book of Proverbs. Just as his grandma, MrJames believes one of the purposes of The Book of Proverbs is to expose readers; particularly the simple, unlearned, foolish, immature and the ignorant to "skillful godly" wisdom from The Most High God—Our Heavenly Father—Supreme Creator—Master Designer of all that exists.

And, the construct, foundation, and structure of Proverbs is to further enhance and increase spiritual growth in the art of living, in the life of the believers who are desiring positive outcomes; and those seeking to know the divine created purpose for their lives. The teachings expounded, repeated, and oftentimes highlighted in the Proverbs, were practiced by Solomon when he was leading God's people and tremendous blessings came to him.

Suddenly, conscious of inner vibrations of sound, it felt as if MrJames LifeCoach heard Grandma saying: "Baby, come closer" because MrJames thinks to himself that he must need to repeat that insight again. Doing so without hesitation, he said it again: "tremendous blessings came to [Solomon] because he asked for, and willingly gave heed to skillful godly wisdom.

Albeit as it is in his inner self, MrJames LifeCoach believe similar blessing can be ours if we also regularly feast upon, willingly glean from, and apply the principles and teachings from the Proverbs to daily lives we will improve our outcomes and performance in the "art of living." In order to emphasize the significance and importance of concentrated reading and study in The Book of Proverbs to you, MrJames LifeCoach reminds the reader of his comprehension that the central theme, gleaned from over five decades of browsing through the Proverbs, is subtly hidden throughout the pages.

MrJames LifeCoach now believes that laced throughout The Book of Proverbs and laid out before the reader, is illuminated highlights of an evidenced-based better way to live. This way of living, if heeded and observed will effectively lead the obedient into becoming better, in an intentional and divine way, at the "Art of Living."

Therefore, consider reading The Book of Proverbs as the ultimate instruction manual for a better way to live, and expecting the application of the principles taught in the Proverbs to begin its transforming influence in your life.

BUT remember, don't quit before the miracle......So let us read, study and share thoughts together with friends and family, as we gather skillful godly wisdom unto ourselves from Proverbs, and decide to willingly observe and cleave unto it.

<u>A thought from MrJames LifeCoach on Proverbs 4:</u>

Cautiously, MrJames LifeCoach points out to readers that there are a few verses in this 4th chapter of The Book of Proverbs that are likely familiar. Actually, some readers may have repeated some of these verses themselves; may have heard them quoted; seen one on a Tee-shirt, bumper sticker, billboard or flashing on a neon sign. Be that as it may be however, it seems only a few of us apply the messages and practice them in daily life. King David, a man after God's own heart, taught the words of these proverbs to his son Solomon.

I now realize that it was Solomon's hearing, heeding and application of his father's words and Godly instructions that blessed his life.

Furthermore, Solomon was not just wise but super abundantly wealthy and well-respected. Be mindful that the skillful Godly wisdom gained from Proverbs is not the same as intellectually knowing; since knowledge can be gained from many sources. In the construct of the reality of today's world, we have virtual access to nearly all of the accumulated knowledge on the planet, literally at our fingertips.

Therefore, instead of doing the thing James instructs the children of God to do: "ask God" (James 1:5), this generation of humanity can just "Ask Google" anything we don't know. But skillful Godly wisdom, on the other hand, comes from a testimony gained from a test or trial of life; sometimes it is successes, failures, and oftentimes navigating through life challenges is what brings skillful Godly wisdom. However, skillful Godly wisdom ONLY comes from the heart, mind, and as the will of God.

Sometimes, MrJames LifeCoach admits, in his busyness to get, earn, and acquire things it is easy to become distracted and lose sight of more important things. Seemingly in the still soft voice of Grandma, Chapter 4 of Proverbs is reminding the reader that: "the main thing is to keep the main thing, the main thing."

Moreover, we are reminded that as we are traveling the life journey do not forget to increase in our understanding of skillful wisdom from God, and all will be well with us in the art of living. Conversely, knowledge, intellect, and just knowing about some things do not make us wise.

However, skillful Godly wisdom is oozing out from the verses of this chapter of Proverbs; and again, there seems to be a reminder to the reader to "seek after skillful godly wisdom." Comparing and equating the gaining of skillful Godly wisdom to be more precious, and more to be desired than rubies, fine gold, and silver.

Furthermore, this chapter also indicate that the seeking after and obtaining of this skillful Godly wisdom brings with its possession; length of days, riches, and honor in the wake and undercurrent as Godly wisdom flows unto the recipient.

Finally, as we decide to observe these instructions, the whisper of Grandma, MrJames, and all throughout this chapter it is suggested that through the art of living these principles; Our Creator "directs our paths" and will lead us to become what we were in fact created to become; accomplishing and fulfilling the full measure of our divinely created purpose.

Remember: He who knows, and knows he knows, is wise. He who knows, and also lives and conducts themselves accordingly is the wiser one. However, he who knows but knows not that he knows is yet still unlearned, immature, and ignorant. But he (she) who knows, and knows he (she) knows; and still conducts themselves, doing things which are contrary to that which they know; they are more foolish.

5
DAY 5 - INVITATION: INCLINE YOUR EAR

PROVERBS 5

Hello readers, hearers, and welcome to any new challenge takers. I thank God for another day above ground with warm blood still going through my veins. Grandma would say as she awakened each day. Today is day five of the Proverbs' daily reading challenge from MrJames LifeCoach.

He invites anyone with a desire to do so to join him and share thoughts and feedback with friends and family as he continues his daily ritual of reading one chapter from Proverbs. Today is the 5th day of the month, and MrJames LifeCoach is reading chapter 5 as he continues his five-year ongoing journey and daily quest of reading from The Book of Proverbs.

MrJames LifeCoach is reading from the New King James and the Amplified Version of the Holy Bible, as well as the New International Version, the New Living Translation, and his often read and preferred King James Version. Grandma always said that the skillful Godly wisdom contained within each chapter of Proverbs is like a gold mine of great worth. Spending time reading from its pages exposes readers to rare nuggets of spiritual insights, "skillful and godly" wisdom from the heart, mind, and directly from the mouth of God. This chapter issues divine warnings, cautions to avoid pitfalls of life, and instructions for becoming better in the art of living.

The Most High God is Our Father, The Supreme Creator, and The Master Designer of all that exists, and HE has hidden precious valuable truths, spiritual insights, and understanding in the Proverb. Openly tucked away from the worldly, especially those who are consumed with fleshly desires preoccupied in the pursuit of wealth above Godly wisdom.

MrJames LifeCoach believes chapter 4 illuminates the understanding of those with real intent, who invest time in reading The Book of Proverbs. It is his testimony that as readers and hearers feed and feast upon these ancient recorded writings and apply these teachings to their daily life, they will be those who will show profound betterment and improved outcomes in the art of living.

Moreover, if this better way to live is observed by readers and hearers, and if whomsoever will, would follow the highlighted pathway, this divine GPS will effectively lead them in creating a better tapestry of outcomes in the "Art of Living."

Therefore, MrJames LifeCoach encourages readers to continue to endure this daily challenge and invest the time to read, study, ponder, and share thoughts together with others as they gather skillful, godly wisdom to themselves, and commit themselves to observe, apply, and cleave unto the teachings of skillful Godly wisdom contained on the pages throughout The Book of Proverbs. In the name of Jesus Christ. Amen.

<u>A thought from MrJames LifeCoach on Proverbs 5:</u>

Immediately, the reader should become aware that the central theme in this 5th chapter of Proverbs is in the form of numerous warnings, cautions, and instructions to avoid, to turn away from, to reconsider, to ponder; and in the chapter, readers and hearers are reminded to forget and cast away some explicitly dangerous, spiritually harmful, and damaging things for the soul. Repeatedly, particular mention is made about the adulteress, and a seductress is a.k.a. the "loose woman."

In chapter 5, MrJames hears the voice of Grandma as an unrelenting voice that is constantly warning readers not to minimize and not forget to give heed to skillful Godly words of wisdom; especially wisdom learned from actual, and oftentimes very costly experiences with eternal consequences.

Furthermore, as MrJames LifeCoach points out, it is suggested in the chapter that the righteous—children of light are to live "soberly, chastely, Godly," and that they are expected to exercise proper discretion, judgment, partiality, and they are to avoid discrimination. Ostensibly, MrJames LifeCoach hears the voice from the pages of chapter 5 as a screaming voice through a megaphone. Although the scream was loud, it sounded like it was the voice of his grandma.

The message from the chapter is that it will be "our own iniquities" that will be the trap used in binding ourselves with "the cords of our sins" and thereby leading us to death. As the unintended outcome due to ignorance, foolishness, lacking discipline and boundaries, and a failure to heed skillful Godly instructions in the art of living.

However, it is repeated again that this skillful godly wisdom ONLY comes from God. Furthermore, this chapter in Proverb goes a bit deeper to further clarify the notion that seeking after, obtaining, possessing, and heeding skillful Godly wisdom will bring divine protection, guidance, riches, honor, and can add days to our lives.

Finally, as suggested in the previous chapter, as we decide to observe the instructions in the Proverbs and through the art of living this better way, the Most High God—Our Heavenly Father, Supreme Creator, and Master Designer of all that exists—"directs our paths" and will lead us to become what we were destined to become. As such, we will accomplish and fulfill the fullness of our divinely created purpose.

In the name of Jesus Christ. Amen.

6

DAY 6 -WARNING: AVOID ADULTERY

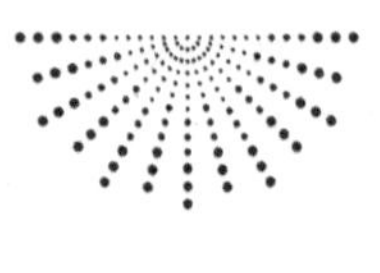

PROVERBS 6

Today is day six of the Proverbs reading challenge issued to readers and hearers by MrJames LifeCoach. If this is your first day to answer the challenge, he welcomes you and urges that you not quit before the miracle. He invites anyone to join him and share their thoughts and feedback, if willing, as he continues his daily ritual of reading a chapter of Proverbs each day as he has continued doing so now for five years.

Reading through chapter 6, he is pondering, reading, gleaning, and commenting based on wording from the King James, New King James, New International Version, New Living Translation, and the Amplified Version of the Holy Bible.

MrJames LifeCoach believes the skillful Godly wisdom and principles, taught within this chapter of Proverbs, can be compared to finding a rare and exquisite diamond mine; but this mine is filled with priceless nuggets, sparkling stones, and boulders of understanding. And when these exposed instructions are applied, they are helpful to lead readers and hearers to becoming better in the art of living; God—Our Heavenly Father—Supreme Creator—Master Designer of all that exists will magnify the understanding of those who continue to read, study, accept, and embrace these words that are saturated with skillful Godly wisdom.

MrJames LifeCoach has mentioned before that if this better way to live is observed, it will effectively lead readers into their divine created purpose; and will improve outcomes in the "Art of Living." Therefore, continue the journey to read, study, accept, embrace, and intentionally attract skillful Godly wisdom into our lives; diligently striving to apply these teachings to our daily rituals of life.

A thought from MrJames LifeCoach on Proverbs 6:

MrJames LifeCoach alerts readers that there seems to be intentional, purposeful, and concentrated efforts of the writer of this chapter, by the use of interpretative sayings, and familiar proverbial language and phrases to reduce ignorance, related to specified matters, to its lowest potential. In this chapter, this is accomplished by using some common words of vernacular to reduce the possibility of readers and hearers of these words of misunderstanding these important messages.

It is so vital, in the art of living, to begin to receive these instructions, that the writer calls attention to seven specific points to take away from this reading. Furthermore, there are also repeated mentions of warnings, cautions, and instructions from the previous chapters. Thus, reiterating the skillful Godly wisdom of avoiding, turning away from, and reconsidering our lustful sinful acts.

Therefore, by the use of multiple and repeated mentions, the writer is further reminding readers not to forget and become entangled by alluring flattery and the alluring perverseness of the seductress and adulteress woman.

Feeling prompted from the eternal realms; cautioned and strongly influenced by Grandma and Grandfather; MrJames LifeCoach was granted approval, permission, and authorization from the world of spirits, allowing him to mention some of the things that are only recorded in this chapter of the Proverbs. And in this chapter only, they are mentioned uncensored, and without a chaser; straightforward and specific; using no uncertain terms.

By the end of reading this chapter, MrJames LifeCoach believes there will be no doubting in the minds of readers that the described actions and behaviors are considered abominations by The Most High God—Our Heavenly Father —The Supreme Creator, and Master Designer of all that exists. Moving forward from this point and throughout the remaining chapters, the described atrocities are only subtly mentioned, implied, or alluded to casually.

However, the potential and associated consequences are extreme, disastrous, unavoidable; can also be eternally damaging; life- altering, and even life-shattering to the art of living canvas.

Therefore, readers and hearers, take heed to avoid, turn away from, rid yourself of, and do not follow after these ways, and the "evil" works of the "flesh" (Gal 5:19-21; 1 John 2:16-17):

1. Pride of life

2. Lying witness

3. Disagreements within the family

4. Wicked planning and thoughts

5. Shedding of innocent blood

6. Swift to do evil

7. A lying tongue

MrJames repeats, reminds, and reiterates to readers and hearers that there is specific mention made about the "loose woman" and about not forgetting to give heed to the words of wisdom, especially the freely accessible exposure to lessons learned from the proverbial School of Hardknocks Academy (www.patreon.com/hardknocks).

In the art of living classroom, these are the elect upper-class lessons learned from hands-on, actual, and practical tutors, but usually, they come with payment that makes them the more costly learning experiences. Furthermore, it is strongly suggested in this chapter and reiterated in a message that came from Grandma; although it was inaudible, it was delivered in a way that was unmistakable and completely understood by MrJames.

In the communication he was prompted, impressed, and encouraged to explain to readers and hearers that the righteous are expected to live "soberly, chaste, and Godly," exercising proper discernment, judgment, and discretion.

MrJames believes, from reading this chapter, that surely it will be plain to see that our own iniquities will trap us, thereby binding ourselves with "the cords of our sins," and in so doing leading ourselves down the pathway to death.

However, MrJames also believes all such unintended outcomes are primarily due to a lack of knowledge, a lack of discipline, a failure to expose ourselves to Proverbs and follow the skillful Godly instructions in the construction in the art of living.

Finally, as MrJames' LifeCoach recollects, it is suggested in the first six chapters already read, and repeated in each chapter at least once; if readers and hearers decide to observe the instructions in The Book of Proverbs, and by applying the teachings in the art of living this better way; The Most High God—Our Heavenly Father, the Supreme Creator—and Master Designer of all that exists will "direct our paths," keeps us away from the evil woman, and will lead us to become what we were preordained and divinely destined to become.

In the construct of our reality, MrJames believes we will be empowered to succeed; blessed and highly favored to accomplish and fulfill our divinely created purpose.

Therefore, with that being said, MrJames asks readers, and hearers as well, a thought-provoking question that is related to the art of living: “Is it accidental, coincidental, or maybe intentional that the cause, theme, and premise of being empowered to succeed, or being bound-up in cords of iniquity is present, consistently, persistently, and continuously repeated all throughout The Book of Proverbs?”

Remember: He who knows and knows he knows is wise. He who knows, lives, and acts according to that which he knows is the wiser. However, he who knows but knows not that he knows is vulnerable; in the art of living he is still ignorant, simple-minded, unlearned, immature, and foolish.

In the name of Jesus Christ. Amen.

7

DAY 7 - WARNING: AVOID FORNICATION [PORN]

PROVERBS 7

Today is the seventh day of The Book of Proverbs reading challenge from MrJames LifeCoach. He invites you to join him every day to read the same appointed chapter from Proverbs that coincides with the date of the month, and then share your thoughts, impressions, and feedback with friends and family. As he continues his daily ritual of reading, MrJames LifeCoach has continued this process for more than five years. He is reading, pondering, and gleaning through the chapters of The Book of Proverbs—a.k.a. The Book of Wisdom using the preferred King James Version, as well as New King James, and the Amplified Version of the Holy Bible.

MrJames describes the skillful and Godly wisdom contained within this chapter of Proverbs, like finding a huge rare and exquisite stone, just by happenstance. The adrenaline rush and "feel Good sensation" he encountered as he read this chapter, he compares it to what a person may experience if they stumble upon a diamond mine, and the mind has an abundant supply of priceless nuggets, and sparkling stones. In his case, MrJames knows the stones found are helpful to lead one to live happy, healthy, and prosperous; and even facilitate the act of becoming better in the art of living.

The Most High God—Our Heavenly Father, Supreme Creator, and Master Designer of all that exists magnifies the insight and understanding of those who are consistent, persistent, and continue to read, study, applying the teachings of Proverbs to their daily lives, and in the construction and art of living a better life.

Again, just as MrJames LifeCoach has mentioned the last three days; if this better way to live is observed, it will effectively lead readers into becoming better at the "Art of Living." Because of that promise he petitions, summons, and invites whomever that are willing to read, study; and will share their thoughts and experiences together; and asks readers and hearers to apply and incorporate this skillful, Godly wisdom and teachings in the art of living life accordingly.

A thought from MrJames LifeCoach on Proverbs 7:

Seemingly, MrJames LifeCoach recognizes, there is a concentrated effort by the writer of chapter 7 of The Book of Proverbs to remove all reasonable doubt associated with the pitfalls of mingling and falling prey to the "immoral woman" and the apparent dangers, and potential spiritual losses that will follow, as the result after becoming seduced by her.

As no other of the Proverbs do, chapter 7 removes all stops and calls the proverbial "spade a spade" and tells the reader that traveling down the road leading in her direction is a spiritual death trap; and the consequences are not to be compared to anything else.

As always, in a manner that is present throughout the Proverbs, MrJames LifeCoach points out to readers that the descriptive language in the chapter is certain, specific, and right to the point; starting with opening words of counsel, guidance, and instruction. As such, there is therefore a decreased possibility of misunderstanding the warnings contained in this important message.

As LifeCoach, and as an accountability partner, MrJames is committed to clients, readers, and hearers to extract from them their highest, best, and a stellar performance in the art of living. Reading this chapter, he becomes aware that there notably, prevalent, and strongly suggested that avoiding the "immoral woman" is critical to the success of the process to excel in the art of living.

Nevertheless, although it may sound as if these first seven chapters and insight from MrJames LifeCoach are heavily religious, restrictive, and not at all respected within the confines of most social circles; these are simple sound standards, and "spiritual principles" upon which to build an intentional and divinely purposeful life.

During these preceding six days of reading Proverbs, this time, the prayers and permeating thoughts of MrJames LifeCoach have been aimed and focused on the art of living. The words of the chapter produced thoughts of how to be the best "you" that "you" can be; how to best utilize the skillful Godly wisdom from Proverbs, and how do lessons learned from personal life experiences facilitate accomplishing that desired end result?

Not certain of the answers to such critically probing and profound questions? MrJames LifeCoach acknowledges that skillful Godly wisdom ONLY comes from The Most High God—Our Heavenly, Supreme Creator, and Master Designer of all that exists. Therefore, listen, observe, think, retain, accept, and embrace the skillful Godly wisdom of the proverbs.

To the readers, MrJames LifeCoach is saying stick around for seven more days; but acknowledging he might just be talking to himself and also knowing from previous readings of the next seven chapters, if need be, he would lock the doors and throw away the keys just to get you to stick around.

MrJames is adamant, primarily because in his experience of reading, studying, and pondering through The Book of Wisdom, he has found that any time invested, devoted, and voluntarily committed to gaining skillful Godly Wisdom, "is time well spent." And in due time, there will always be a return on the investment; and returns will be more valuable than silver or gold.

Finally, MrJames reminds you again: God—Our Heavenly Father, Our Creator, Supreme Being, and Master Designer of all that exists "directs our paths" and will lead us to become what we were destined to become. And as such, we will accomplish and fulfill our divinely created purpose. Ask yourself: Why is this promise continuously repeated all throughout the Proverbs?

Remember: He who knows and knows he knows is wise. He who knows and lives and conducts themselves according to what he knows is the wiser. However, he who knows but knows not that he knows is yet vulnerable, simple-minded, still unlearned, immature, ignorant, and foolish.

In the name of Jesus Christ. Amen.

8
YOU ARE UNIQUE, WONDERFULLY MADE

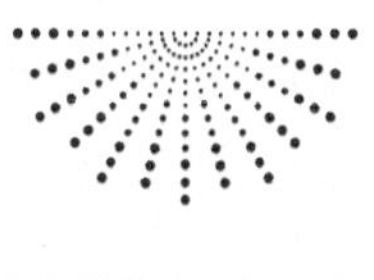

WEEK ONE

Suddenly, MrJames LifeCoach was awakened, in the middle of the night, before he was to begin sharing insights for this eighth day and the start of the second week. Deep inside, he had the strong sense that Grandma had called his name and felt for sure in his inner self that she was present in his room.

In his now conscious awareness, it was so real and reminiscent of being awakened by Grandma. As she had done so many times when YoungMan had been awakened by Grandma to help her in with something in their garden or to go with her on a trip to help her handle some business somewhere.

Fully awake and sitting on the side of the bed, he realized he was alone in his room. Just as suddenly as he had been awakened, he began to sense between his ears and see behind his eyes on the screen of his mind what seemed to be words coming into his focused awareness.

In shock and awe, he could see the words from a poem Grandma had written for him when he was struggling in the art of living; confused and battling with f.r.o.g.s. of life and not knowing what to do. Amazingly, in the wee hours of the morning on this eighth day, he could hear the voice of Grandma saying to him to let the readers and hearers of this message on Proverbs know this about themselves.

In her still soft voice, she began repeating these words as MrJames LifeCoach was reading them from the screen of his mind: "Life, even with all of its twists and turns, still continues to be unfolding undoubtedly just as planned by the Most High God—Our Heavenly Father, the Supreme Creator, and Master Designer of Heaven, Earth, and all that exists. Recognize that all life experiences have made you, me, and them who we are today. And, if any facet of life were left out or changed, none of us would be the sum total of who we are as we begin this second week of reading these Proverbs."

Then Grandma continued: "Each reader and hearer of these words today are: rare, exquisite, unique, valuable, and wonderfully made. A precious child of the Most High God; put here on this earth with a created purpose. A purpose that includes being endowed with genuine love and adoration for art of living and for the experience of this life's journey.

Remember first and foremost, as we (Grandma is always there) begin this season of life and the second week of their investment into themselves: we are all a child of the most high God and was created by the Creator of heaven and earth. There is a great purpose for which each of HIS children were created to fulfill."

MrJames heard the inaudible voice of Grandma distinctly say: "Baby," and through these words, this time he knew Grandma was also speaking to all readers, hearers, and challenge keepers. Grandma said: "The adversary, Lucifer the Devil—Satan is like a roaring lion, standing in the shadows, and from behind the bushes he roars. In the open, we would all see our adversary is but a defanged pussycat; but he goes about seeking whomsoever he may hinder and frighten; deceive, delay, detour, and detract from their created purpose.

It is true, the created purpose of the adversary of humanity is only to steal peace and hope; kill dreams and ambitions; and to destroy structure, foundation, purpose, and divine destiny." Coming from the sacred corner, the set apart closet, and the sanctified chamber of the mind of Grandma, MrJames was hearing out loud, for the first time her vocal voice from the eternal realm vibrating sounds in his ears. Grandma was praying for MrJames, just as she often would; but this time Grandma was praying for all readers and the hearers of this sacred message about the Proverbs.

These are the words Grandma prayed: "It is my prayer that not any of them would continue to be counted amongst his captives and casualties; Heavenly Father, I am now asking, for the purpose of escaping the grasps, traps, and cords of wickedness; I now desire further insight, guidance, light, and knowledge be given to all readers and hearers.

As we voluntarily begin this second week of exposure to The Book of Wisdom; as these readers and hearers continue to meditate on the art of living; realistically considering the dangers, the adversarial trials, and the real-life challenges ahead; that they may ponder the purpose and meaning of each life experience. Heavenly Father, grant that they may be filled with an increased desire to become, and be divinely persuaded to believe; that all readers and hearers in the art of living, may become that unto which they were created, foreordained and destined to become, according to the spiritual blueprint of their divine purpose."

MrJames begins to notice that daylight is beginning to break through the cloak of darkness, and the prior undetectable dawning of the eighth day; is approaching across the horizon. Grandma continues to pray for readers and hearers; boldly saying: "Heavenly Father, it is my belief, surely the spirits of Goodness and Mercy shall continue to follow the devoted, committed, and consistent readers throughout all the remaining days of their lives, as they continue to invest time in themselves."

Then MrJames heard Grandma say: "Heavenly Father, I pray that the Highly blessed favor of those spirits shall overtake them, hedge up the way around them, and guide them that they may not procrastinate, not put-off, and not offend God —Our Heavenly Father, the Supreme Creator, an Master Designer of all that exists."

Hearing the praying words of Grandma, MrJames began thinking to himself, and saying out Loud: "I might just be talking to myself" but in his mind he knew Grandma had been speaking on behalf of, and for the present and future benefit of all readers and hearers. Moving forward from that present moment, MrJames LifeCoach began to express his gratitude and gratefulness for the blessings of his life on this planet; for his knowledge of the true purpose of life; for the certainty of his testimony of the Lord Jesus Christ, as his personal Savior.

Realizing that the presence, influence, and the conscious awareness of Grandma was fading back into the invisible realm; MrJames LifeCoach began to pray; asking forgiveness for poor choices, unrighteous judgments, sins, shortcomings, and asking that the consequences of my actions would not be a spiritual, mental, psychological, sociological, nor financial hindrance unto those in the circle of influence around me.

Furthermore, my prayer is that readers and hearers not continue to be blinded by the cunning deceitfulness of adversarial friends, empts, minions, and the wicked associates of the enemy. I remind readers and hearers of the cautions within the first week reading of Proverbs; some natural human emotions, knee-jerk reactions, and destructive addictive behaviors are especially difficult to master or control; particularly emotions, reactions, and behaviors that are deeply rooted in traumatizing, humiliating, disappointing incidents, and stressful circumstances of distant and even not so distant past.

Albeit as that may be; from my personal experiences; from the teachings of Grandma; and from the structure and foundation of exposure to the Proverbs; it has become the belief of MrJames LifeCoach that there is a way to be released from the grips and influences of the past on future emotions, actions, and behaviors.

First, acknowledge the existence of these influences.

Second, admit personal "powerlessness & unmanageability" over the effects of those influences and remain forever mindful that this world is controlled by eternal governing laws. Sometimes referred to as "the law of cause and effect or sewing and reaping."

Third, admit and accept that nothing is fortunate or unfortunate on the Earth plane as we travel the highways in the art of living in this life. Grandma taught MrJames LifeCoach this absolute truth; that it is our perspective that gives meanings to the happenings in our lives.

Furthermore, it is my belief that The Most High God—Our Heavenly Father, the Supreme Creator, and Master Designer of all that exists is in control of all things. Grandma always reminded me, saying to me; "Baby, mind you now, I did not say HE controls just those things we perceive as good; but just as Proverbs teaches us; HE controls all things (the perceived good, the bad, and the indifferent), and all things work together for HIS perceived good; and for those who love God and are called and created according to His purposes (Rom 8:28).

Keeping that in mind, admit that there is in fact not a right way to do a WRONG thing; and incorporate a desire to do that which is right and most effective into your efforts to become released from the paralyzing grips, and negative influences of the past; that you may soar into your future on the wings, the structure, and the foundation of teachings from The Book of Wisdom and the Proverbs.

More than five years ago, MrJames LifeCoach began his concentrated quest, search, pursuit, and seeking after skillful Godly wisdom to augment, enhance, and add to his desire to forever and always be an instrument of good in the hands of The Most High God.

However, consequences of poor choices, errors in judgments and reaping what has been sown, have been overflowing, illuminating, highlighting, and influencing his life choices in the art of living on the sketched pathway of a preordained—thought-out beforehand blueprint of his divinely purposed life.

You, me, all readers and hearers; as individuals we are One-of-a-kind: A rare, unique, wonderfully made creation. There is not another person, exactly like me, or you in the history of mankind; nor will there ever be. The Most High God—Our Heavenly Father, the Supreme Creator, and Master Designer of all that exists, has made me and you valuable; one of a kind in all of creation.

Therefore, MrJames LifeCoach seeks wisdom from The Book of Proverbs; Holy Bible, Sacred Scriptures, Prophets and Apostles; inspired Teachers; and from the Spirit of Knowledge; the Spirit of Insight; the Spirit of Understanding; the Spirit of Revelation; and the Spirit of TRUTH.

I am seeking the presence and conscious awareness of the still soft Voice; from the eternal realms of heaven; that it may come to enlighten the mind and reveal the good, acceptable, and perfect will of the Lord (Rom 12:2) for the outcomes from the challenge I have issued to readers, hearers, and all those who will rise-up, and come forward to accept this art of living challenge.

Heavenly Father, so that the Spirit be not grieved; unrestrained and unhindered; I ask forgiveness for any impure thoughts, actions or deeds, and seek the companionship of the Holy Ghost to penetrate the daily lives, and righteous affairs of readers and hearers; and renew a right Spirit unto *me*.

In the name of Jesus Christ. Amen.

9
DAY 8 - SKILLFUL GODLY WISDOM

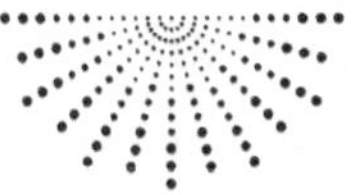

PROVERBS 8

Today is day eight. As some readers are just beginning to read, on the second week reading the chapter from Proverbs each day that coincides with the date of the month; after a challenge and an invitation was issued by MrJames LifeCoach and all readers and hearers were welcomed to join with him.

For some readers and hearers, this may be your first day; as he has invited each of you who so desires to do so, may share your thoughts and feelings on Facebook @ MrJames LifeCoach; www.patreon.com/hardknocks; and with family, friends, fellow Christian believers, and non-believers.

MrJames continues his daily ritual of reading from Proverbs each day; this process he has continued now for more than five years. MrJames is pondering, reading, gleaning, commenting, and sharing his insights, impressions, and feelings based on wording from his preferred translation; which is also Grandma's favorite translation; the King James Version, as well as New King James, New International Version; New Living Translation; and the Amplified Version of the Holy Bible.

Some may ask, "What is the Art of Living?" MrJames LifeCoach describes the art of living as simply the determination to continue moving and pushing forward in your quest of living to become what you were created to become; no matter what life may throw at you along the way.

The art of living demands the individual to embrace and internalize a life perspective that incorporates a basic belief in the existence of an Eternal Creator—The Most High God —Our Heavenly Father, Supreme Creator, and Master Designer of ALL that exists.

MrJames LifeCoach believes, because newborn infants are not delivered with an instruction manual attached, that it is an absolute truth that C.S. Lewis appropriately explained; when he stated: "Life is lived forward [one day at a time], but life is understood backwards" when we stop to ponder, to review, and to reflect on past life experiences.

Therefore, as LifeCoach I accept also as an absolute truth, that our daily life experiences are tailor-made with a divine purpose and meaning interwoven into the fabric of the experience. As such, the essence of the art of living is to gain useful, skillful, and Godly wisdom from ALL of our daily interactions and experiences. Nevertheless, all too often on our life journey, before we begin to walk in our divinely created purpose, it is oftentimes later rather than sooner in life when we come to realize and acknowledge we are getting "too soon old, and too late smart" in the construct and make-up of our reality; and, in the art of living.

A thought from MrJames LifeCoach on Proverbs 8:

Moving on from this point, and keeping all those previously mentioned things in mind, MrJames realizes this chapter of Proverbs has an undeniable and insistent message to seek after "skillful godly wisdom" and that beckoning call has a distinct presence that is proclaimed within all chapters of Proverbs. The emphasis of The Book of Proverbs, although canonized, revered, and consecrated as sacred Scripture; the proverbs themselves are not just religious tenets.

However, the insights put forth from MrJames, they are also those that were displayed in the life of Grandma. Because of reading through Proverbs for more than five years; MrJames desires that the insights be received as if coming forth from the eternal realms; and as an earnest appeal to readers and hearers to consider the existence of an unseen spiritual aspect to our physical existence.

In other words, MrJames believes that absolutely nothing happens in this world by accident, coincidence, or by random chance, happenstance, nor by that demon called "**luck**" (Prov 16:33). MrJames believes that the determining factors, and the governing influences on outcomes could be labeled as the laws we know as "cause and effect" (Galatians 6:7-9); the laws of choices and consequences (D&C 130:20-21); or sewing and reaping only what has been sown.

However, from a strict scientific perspective it could be explained as act vs react (psychology); or action vs reaction (physics); and in chemistry described as **act-ing** and being **act-ed-upon** (D&C 58:27-29; 2 Ne 2:14-17). In other words, it is as if I can hear Grandma saying: "Baby, come here a little closer; you not gonna go out there planting corn, and be expecting to pick tomatoes; its just not gonna happen."

MrJames LifeCoach believes Proverbs teaches readers and hearers about the absolute and eternal laws relating to the existence of an invisible and also irrevocable, inalterable, and unchanging link to outcomes (D&C 130:20-21). He also believes; the link lies within the words we express daily; our daily choices; our actions and behaviors; as well as desired and undesired outcomes. It is in the art of living, and the lessons learned from the school of hard knocks that Proverbs fittingly establishes that within such as these are the places where the link resides.

The intent of the challenge issued by MrJames LifeCoach is to share milk, crumbs, and pebbles of knowledge and insights with some readers and hearers who answer the challenge. Likewise, LifeCoach desires to introduce and pass along to other committed and devoted readers and hearers; golden nuggets, rocks, and stones for the foundation and structure of their pathway to positive outcomes, and the roadway to a better way to live.

Ultimately, the desire of MrJames LifeCoach is to fill the full measure of his divinely created purpose; which is to blaze a trail through the wilderness of mortality and the frogs of life; from his perspective as he has spent time as A #1 Knucklehead; and after being immersed in, but also graduating from the School of Hardknocks Academy experiences. And, I must admit doing so, certified with honors (Lol). However, after this first week, I know I might just be talking to myself.

Grandma (Ma'Dear or Inez), Grandfather (Richard), and my three most revered Great, Great Grandmas (Postoria, Sarah, and Acenie); Great Auntie' (Buelah, Gladys, Bernice, and Jessie Mae); all are significant contributors to the construction of the blazed trail left by them for MrJames LifeCoach to follow.

And, because of honoring the commitment made by him to his Grandmas, grandfather, and others in the eternal realms, including Jr Frog; and by reading through Proverbs; MrJames came to understand why Grandma said: "Baby, do not tell them everything."

It is because all Guardian Angels only speak and confirm truth—they do not force your obedience or your acceptance; nor force your application of the truth in the art of living. Neither will Guardian Angels force application of eternal truth into your life.

MrJames knows for certain that Guardian Angels will insistently encourage, gently persuade, and will always be prayerfully and fully expecting of obedience, However, MrJames testifies of the truth that Guardian Angels all patiently waited for him to voluntarily choose for himself to knock, ask for (James 1:5; John 14:14), and seek after (Matt 7:7-8) skillful Godly wisdom; in his own time.

Godly Wisdom, not an abundance of knowledge and useless worldly facts, is what is needed and necessary to give birth to, propagate, produce, and bring forth positive outcomes in the art of living. **SHE—WISDOM must be pursued, sought after, looked for, and found; as he who finds a wife—SHE finds favor with God.** Likewise, he (she) who finds wisdom —SHE will conceive in the art of living tapestry and portrait of his (her) life, the favor of The Most High God—Our Heavenly Father, Supreme Creator, and Master Designer of all that exists.

However, in all thy getting, understand this (Prov 4:7): for Godly wisdom to be transferred from the eternal realms of existence; received, perceived, internalized and manifested in the physical realm; understood behind the eyes and between the ears; she— WISDOM only passes through Sacred higher points and portals of divinely authorized passageways. Grandma and MrJames LifeCoach has found that one such passageway is labeled: The Book of Proverbs—a.k.a. The Book of Wisdom.

MrJames LifeCoach has gained, from his Grandma, Guardian Angels—other grandparents, descendants in the eternal realms; and from his time invested in the study of Proverbs; unique insights and perspectives on science, religion, spirituality; and the interconnectedness that is inherent to all three disciplines. Readers and hearers answering his challenge are being guided along with him through a pathway of life lessons, in the art of living, by a plethora— host of Guardian Angels unknowingly present in our daily life experiences.

These strategically placed Guardian facilitators and Divine guides in the art of living, helps us along using the blueprint —map of our divinely created life purpose. It is obvious to MrJames, behind his eyes and between his ears, elect and select readers and hearers who stand up to his challenge of investing time in themselves will also be favored to follow the blazed trail to drink from the fountain of skillful Godly wisdom.

In so doing this, they will reap more positive outcomes in the art of living; become more fully focused on living according to their divine purpose; and, just as MrJames has done, they will become more accepting of all life experiences.

Building on the structure and foundation of the existence of The Most High God—Our Heavenly Father, Supreme Creator, and Master Designer of all that exists is truth. A Sovereign God in absolute control of all things; and, readers and hearers, through the application of insights, knowledge, and understanding from Proverbs; will begin to see on the screen of their mind behind their eyes, and hear and feel between their ears; that in the art of living, ALL life experiences are beneficial in some positive way to that process (Isaiah 55:8)

Therefore, when life happens, Grandma would say: "It is what it is" and then she got busy to minimize the effects and make the best of the situation; no matter what life-challenges may manifest in life's pathway. MrJames, readers and hearers must need to continue moving forward in the art of living, and in the construction of their reality from the perspective of the divine; and in accordance with skillful Godly wisdom.

As MrJames is approaching the end of day eight, the still soft voice of Grandma begins to warmly penetrate the silence.

It is as if her voice was riding into his conscious awareness on a ray of sunshine, just as the sun is setting on the horizon and piercing through the kitchen window from the outside, and shining on the table where he is working. MrJames, perceiving a sense of serenity it was as if he could feel a warm and fuzzy embrace, and could heard her gentle, inaudible beckoning call: "Baby, you need to explain to readers and hearers about that impression of insight that came through to both of us when you were frantic, emotionally hysterical, and psychologically traumatized during your f.r.o.g.s. dilemma. Remember, it was my sister; your great-aunt Beulah from the eternal realms that came to sit with you, and she explained to you that everything happens for a reason" …(Then….total silence) Grandma was gone again….

For now, MrJames just strongly encourages each of you on this eighth day of the challenge; and he urges, craves, beseeches, and pleads with you to read this Proverb for yourself. Hear this message in your voice; behind your own eyes and from between your own ears.

In its entirety, this chapter answers questions about HOW to be the best you that you can be in the art of living? WHY readers and hearers should seek after and establish a prominent prioritized place for skillful Godly wisdom in the art of living? WHY and HOW is it that the skillful Godly wisdom of Proverbs serves as guide, and can somehow steer readers so that they may avoid some of life's pitfalls?

Finally, MrJames welcomes new challenge takers; and reminds other readers and hearers again: The Most High God—Our Eternal Heavenly Father, Supreme Creator, and Master Designer of all that exists "directs our paths" and will lead us to become what we were destined to become; and we will accomplish, and fulfill our divinely created purpose.

Remember: He (or she) who knows and knows he (or she) Knows, is the wise. He (or she) who knows, lives, and conducts themselves according to what he (or she) knows, are the wiser.

However, he (or she) who knows but knows not that he (or she) knows, they are yet vulnerable, simple-minded, still unlearned, immature, ignorant, and foolish.

In the name of Jesus Christ. Amen.

10

DAY 9 - BEGINNING OF WISDOM

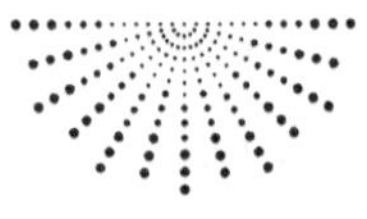

PROVERBS 9

Today is day nine of reading a chapter from Proverbs every day; a challenge issued by MrJames LifeCoach. Anyone who desires is welcomed to join with him each day through these writings to share thoughts, impressions, feelings, and feedback with family and friends. For over five years, he has continued this daily ritual of reading the chapter from The Book of Proverbs—a.k.a. The Book of Wisdom—that coincides with the date of the month.

His shared insights, impressions, and comments are from his preferred Bible translation King James Version, and four other favorites: New King James, New International, New Living Translation, and Amplified Versions of the Holy Bible.

C.S. Lewis explained, "Life is lived forward" one day at a time, "but life is understood backwards" when we stop and reflect on our past experiences. Therefore, MrJames accepts as reality that our daily life experiences, including challenges and pleasantries, are tailor-made with either a divine lesson, a purpose, or a meaning that is interwoven into the experience.

Primarily, the essence of the art of living is the gaining of useful, skillful, and Godly wisdom from daily life, and from various other social interactions and experiences The art of Living requires the individual to consider, embrace, and internalize a life perspective that will encompass and combine with a basic core belief that there exists a Supreme Eternal Creator—God—Master Designer of all that exists.

However, it turns out that all too often most of us will not begin to embrace our divinely created purpose sooner on the landscape of life, but usually it is later in the span of our life journey when we eventually come to realize we are getting too soon old, but too late smart.

A thought from MrJames LifeCoach on Proverbs 9:

Keeping those aforementioned thoughts in mind, after having read Proverbs before, MrJames recognizes this is the shorter of all the Proverb chapters. The length of the chapter is not an indicator of a lack of significance of the subject matter addressed by the writer. The single focus of the skillful Godly wisdom of this chapter is directed on the social stratification of skillful Godly wisdom as feminine; and "she" is so described throughout all thirty-one chapters.

MrJames LifeCoach believes the questions Grandma would ask him about this chapter would be: What is the male equal to skillful Godly wisdom? Will both the male and female components be required to be embraced in a relationship with each other in order to produce a life of divine purpose?

The Most High God—Our Eternal Heavenly Father—Supreme Creator, and Master Designer of all that exists is The Male component, Jesus Christ—His Son is a Male component; and The Holy Ghost—He (John 14:26) is a Male component.

MrJames LifeCoach believes this chapter makes it crystal clear that the absence of skillful Godly wisdom—HER, the female component of physical and spiritual conception; that which produces positive outcomes in the art of living will be effectively hindered. As the result of that absence, individuals are left to their "own understanding" and they will be barren in spiritual strength; unable to produce spiritual fortitude.

A professional building contractor friend of MrJames compares it to constructing a building on a sandy foundation; and when the wind and storms come against that structure all you will have left is a pile of rubble.

Similarly, the results in the art of living will be the same, just as alluded to in this chapter. When the winds and storms of life come there will be life-shattering consequences. MrJames believes a person's failure to voluntarily invest time to seek for, and find skillful Godly wisdom; at the end of the day; the results will be no real lasting, authentic, and sustainable spiritual increase.

Besides that, the best outcomes to expect in that person's art of living; and in the life of this person will be secular, worldly, and at its best it will only be intellectual philosophy of men. Grandma said: "To God; our worldly knowledge does not amount to the cost of a hill of beans in his eyes; and man's intellect and insights are as noticeable to God as the ripple effects from dropping a thimble full of water into the ocean; insignificant and inconsequential in comparison.

The knowledge from the world is considered "foolishness to God" (Isa 55:8-10); as such there will be little to no spiritual conception from following the world's concepts and precepts in the art of living. In other words; intellect, mental fortitude; nor worldly insights, knowledge, and secular understanding will not sustain the person in the art of living who lacks skillful Godly wisdom.

Thus, as implied in this chapter, apart from skillful Godly wisdom fulfillment and becoming a reflection of the blueprint of an individual's divinely created life purpose in the art of living, is probably unlikely. According to the writers of Proverbs, and as it was taught by King Solomon, skillful Godly wisdom only comes from God; as a gift granted from God.

Furthermore, in this short chapter it is not the subject alone that has intrigued and piqued the interest of MrJames, but it is the fact that several verses of the 9th chapter of Proverbs is repeated over and over throughout all the other thirty chapters; making it pristine and crystal clear that an investment of your time focused and in search of gaining skillful Godly wisdom is the most effective way to produce positive, long-term, sustainable outcomes in the art of living.

Therefore, MrJames encourages individuals to read the Proverbs for themselves; primarily it is because he was cautioned, warned, and restrained by Grandma; to not tell readers and hearers everything; not to just re-state or copy Proverbs; and not to heavily quote the Proverbs in this work.

Grandmas, who are Guardian Angels of MrJames, now in the eternal realms, unanimously said: "Baby, you have been well prepared in the art of living. You are now ready to fill the full measure of your divine purpose; and you are to go forth and become the reflection of the blueprint of your created purpose; and share any insights you have gained along the pathway of your life and from reading through Proverbs."

Then, MrJames heard the words again: "Baby, come closer; before I leave you for this assigned time." Feeling surprised by her comment, before thinking I asked: Grandma, what do you mean this assigned time? She quickly said to me: "Baby, at this time I can only say that you are well prepared. But it is time for you to know, that as Guardian Angels we were assigned to watch over you so that you would not slip, stumble, and fall into the abyss.

However, we did not prepare you, or get you ready for your life purpose; it was your tailor-made life experiences, life-shattering, world-shaking experiences with f.r.o.g.s. of life that has you fully prepared for the upcoming and unfolding of your preordained, created life purpose.

Remember, everything happens for a reason in the art of living on the Earth plane. You are a stellar student Baby. The student is ready and so the TEACHER of wisdom will appear. Get ready! Get ready! Get ready!" …..(total silence)…..

In total shock over Grandma's words, MrJames was not consciously aware immediately that she was gone again. In his closing comments about this short, effective, and impactful chapter; MrJames LifeCoach decided not to identify repetitive topics in the short chapter. However, included in this chapter is mentioned the sources of major life pitfalls, heartaches, hindrances in the art of living our divinely created purpose.

MrJames insists that the emphasis of The Book of Proverbs is not religious, as he has stated before. Instructions and insights contained within are an appeal to readers and hearers to consider that there is a significant unseen aspect to our physical existence. Moreover, there is a link that is present in our choices, our actions, our conduct, and our behaviors that produce desired and undesired outcomes in our lives. The message through this chapter, although short and direct, is also sharp and can be piercing to the soul.

Again, MrJames welcomes any new challenge takers and asks all readers and hearers to read this Proverb for yourself; to identify the repeated instructions; to hear and receive the messages chapter 9 sends to you. Then, ask yourself: how do you make use of these insights to assist you in the art of living and becoming the best you that you possibly are created to become? And if we do all that we can do, trust that all things do work together so we will accomplish and fulfill the full measure of our divine created purpose.

Remember: He (or she) who knows and knows he (or she) knows is wise. He (or she) who knows and lives and conducts themselves according to what he (or she) knows is the wiser. However, he (or she) who knows but knows not that he knows is yet vulnerable, simple-minded, still unlearned, immature, ignorant, and foolish. There is not a right way to do a wrong thing.

In the name of Jesus Christ. Amen.

11

DAY 10 - HEART OF THE MATTER

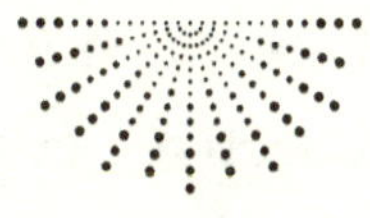

PROVERBS 10

Today is the tenth consecutive day of reading a chapter from Proverbs, if you accepted the challenge issued by MrJames LifeCoach at the beginning of the month. Anyone is welcomed who desires to read the chapter each day that coincides with the date of the month; preferably one each and every day; one a day for thirty-one days; or occasionally read at least one corresponding chapter any day you may desire. MrJames LifeCoach has been engaging this daily commitment to read a chapter of Proverbs each day for five years.

The initial aim, goal, and focus of this challenge is for readers and hearers to establish whether you understand, believed in, accept as absolute truth and if you can explain and liken the concept of: "divinely created purpose" to your specific individual life.

The Art of Living requires the individual to consider, embrace, and internalize a life perspective that incorporates an absolute belief that there exist a Sovereign—Supreme—Eternal Creator—God—Master Designer of all that exists.

Therefore, the belief that each and "everything happens for a reason" leads to a belief that there is no such thing as a true accident—nothing unintended, unforeseen, or unexpected from the spiritual perspective, ever really happens. The eternal laws of cause and effects are forever and always the ruling and governing authority (D&C 130:20-21). Therefore, MrJames LifeCoach accepts as absolute truth, daily life experiences are tailor-made; specific to the individual; and all life experiences encountered has divine purpose and meaning interwoven into those experiences.

The essence of the art of living is to gain useful, skillful, Godly wisdom from daily experiences and social interactions. MrJames explains: "Sometime I have to talk to myself; saying look-er-here self we need to talk."

Nevertheless, most of us do not immediately embrace our divinely created purpose because it is usually later on in the timeline of life; in hindsight, is when we begin to ponder, reflect, review, and even reminisce our past life experiences. Then, that is for some of us, we begin to realize we are getting "too soon old, and too late smart" in the art of living as we are traveling in the "wilderness" spread across the pathway of our life course journey.

<u>A thought from MrJames LifeCoach on Proverbs 10:</u>

Keeping those things front in mind; after having read The Book of Proverbs before, MrJames LifeCoach recognizes this chapter begins to draw a distinct proverbial line in the sand. As a loving father speaks to his son, Solomon's words precisely describe, separates, and compares life outcomes of the wicked—traveling in darkness; against outcomes of the righteous—walking in the light.

Although it is somewhat subtly; in this proverb, Solomon is suggesting to readers and hearers that spiritual "knowledge" is spiritual "power" and that phrase could properly summarize this chapter.

Solomon's emphasis to readers and hearers, reiterates that skillful Godly wisdom is to be valued, desired, pursued; and applied if readers and hearers are to produce a life of positive outcomes and divine purpose in the art of living.

Furthermore, within the chapter there are three or four phrases and topics (identify them), that are repeated over and over. MrJames believes this repetition should be understood as Solomon's way to imply significant importance to those instructions, well worth readers and hearers' additional efforts, cautions, and that consideration should be given to observe, to accept, and obey.

MrJames decides not to identify the phrase nor the topics, but the writer mentioned some of the sources of life's major pitfalls, heartaches, and hindrances to the art of living our divine Created purpose. MrJames takes the position that these insights, emphasized by Solomon in The Book of Proverbs—The Book of Wisdom, are meant to be received as a passionate appeal to incite, pique, and raise interest in the audience; asking readers and hearers to seriously consider the unseen cause and effect connection to our physical existence.

In its essence, the chapter is declaring quite loudly: "judge things not according to the appearance" (John 7:24); putting forth a perspective in the art of living that suggest there is a link present in our daily choices; actions, conduct, and our behaviors that will produce both; pleasant and unpleasant; and desired and undesired outcomes along the pathways of our lives.

As stated before (repetition is important), the underlying and ultimate intent of the MrJames LifeCoach is to encourage readers and hearers to read; not just this chapter, but all of The Book of Proverbs; especially this chapter, and the previous two. However, do so specifically to identify for yourself, somewhere behind your eyes and between your ears; those repeated instructions, and to receive the inspired messages of each chapter. MrJames believes the message received will be specific to the individual; just as it was for him. Nevertheless, your message may be unique and altogether different.

As MrJames was concluding reading this chapter, he felt as if he had been ushered into the presence, and was under the shadowing influence of Grandma again. In her now familiar but inaudible voice, accompanied by a relaxing and refreshing sensation; Grandma whispered to MrJames from the realms of eternity, into the physical plane of his current reality (Omg, he thinks to himself. I wish I knew how she does that).

And the message received from the essence of her being, brought to his mind to ask readers and hearers what MrJames had had no thought to ask: "Baby, ask them how they will make use of these insights; and upcoming insights to assist them in the art of living, walking in the light to become a reflection of the blueprint of their divine created purpose, and become the best person they could?"....(Again, total silence).... In the flash of the moment, Grandma was gone again.....

Finally, as he ends reading through this chapter, MrJames LifeCoach reminds readers and hearers again; and welcomes all first day challenge takers; Saying to all: "The Most High God—Our Eternal Heavenly Father—Supreme Creator—Master Designer of all that exists "directs our paths" and will lead us, as we submit to his will (Mosiah 3:19).

Thus, as Solomon clearly suggests, the choices we make each day are significant and instrumental in the divine process; in the art of living; and serves to enable or hinder the pathway leading us to become what we were destined to become.

Accordingly, as this chapter seems to suggest; in the art of living if we do all that we can, trusting that "all things do work together for the good" (Rom 8:28), we will not only fulfill and accomplish our foreordained purpose; but in the process we shall become a reflection of the eternal blueprint of our predestined divine life purpose.

Remember: He (or she) who knows and knows he (or she) knows is wise. He (or she) who knows and lives and conducts themselves according to what he (or she) knows is the wiser. However, he (or she) who knows but knows not that he knows is yet vulnerable, simple-minded, still unlearned, immature, ignorant, and foolish. You are getting too soon old, and too late smart. Getting so much the older, but getting no better; keep living like you are living, and you just get old; then, you just die. There is not a right way to do a wrong thing.

In the name of Jesus Christ. Amen.

12

DAY 11 - SELF-PERVERTING SPEECH

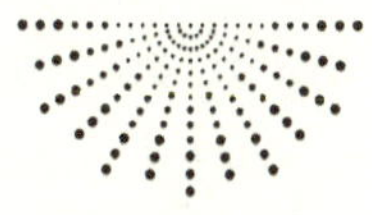

PROVERBS 11

It is now the eleventh consecutive day reading or listening to one chapter from The Book of Proverbs—The Book of Wisdom, as a challenge issued by MrJames LifeCoach. He invited whomsoever to join him reading every day and share insights, thoughts, impressions, and feedback (www.patreon.com/hardknocks) as he continues his daily task of reading the chapter from Proverbs that coincide with the date of the month; a process he has continued doing for over five years.

"What is the Art of Living?" The Art of Living is simply the determination to continue pushing forward in your quest to become what you were created to. The Art of Living requires the individual to consider, embrace, and internalize a life perspective that incorporates a belief that there exists an Eternal Heavenly Father—Supreme Creator—God—Master Designer of all that exists. Therefore, under HIS Sovereign control, "everything happens for a reason" and there is no such thing as an accident—nothing, absolutely nothing unintended, unforeseen, or unexpected ever happens in this world.

As such, all daily life experiences; including pleasant and not so pleasant; especially earth-shaking and life- shattering ones; ALL are tailor-made to the individual with a divine life-lesson, purpose and meaning interwoven into the actual reality of the experience; social interactions, association, or communication.

Nevertheless, usually it is later in the span of our life, when some of us come to acknowledge we are getting "too soon old, and too late smart" as the sands of life pass through the hourglass, and the waters of life pass slow and gradually under the bridge of destiny.

A thought from MrJames LifeCoach on Proverbs 11:

MrJames recognizes this chapter continues in making a comparison between outcomes in the lives of the wicked against outcomes in the lives of the righteous. After five years; he also believes there is no other way to interpret the meaning from this chapter; except to accept the pages from the previous chapters, as the evidence-based proof; and personal testimonials from wise King Solomon as truth. The chapter is confirming that the wicked will not escape punishment; but also assures the righteous that they will come out ahead in the long run. Readers and hearers are just "stuck on stupid" students in A #1 Knucklehead University, or attending art of living School of Hardknocks Academy; all other readers who browse the chapter should consider the words of this Proverb as Guardian Angels; shining forth from the eternal realms.

The words of this chapter and the art of living challenge radiates as illuminating lights of divine knowledge, insights, understanding, and instructions. **Useful** for brightening the baffling, dark, and perplexing places that are cunningly covering and concealing the pathway leading to the blueprint of our foreordained divine destiny.

Grandma only had 3rd grade formal education; but one of her favorite sayings was: "knowledge is power" and that could be the theme and summary for this chapter; because knowledge, understanding, and skillful godly wisdom—"she" must be desired, looked for, and pursued if readers and hearers are to produce a life reflecting a divine purpose.

As MrJames recalls how Grandma would sometimes caution him; he talks to himself, saying: "Look-er-here self—readers and hearers also; we must need to talk" and on this eleventh day, he said, as words of caution to readers and hearers: "Do not be deceived; wickedness can and "never will be happiness" (Alma 41:10).

As MrJames comes to the end of reading this chapter; as he closes the Bible he takes away with him; behind his eyes and between his ears; knowledge, insight, and understanding from his study of The Book of Proverbs: There is not a right way to do a wrong thing; ill-gotten gain will not be profitable; and to them who initially reap its benefits, time and the Godly wisdom oozing from the Proverbs seem to confirm that in the long-term cheaters never win.

Once again, MrJames encourages each reader and hearer; especially welcoming those answering the challenge and this is your first day; read this chapter of Proverbs for yourself; identify your specific meaningful instructions; and the instructions, words, and phrases; especially the ones repeated in the chapter.

"Baby come closer" he heard the words seemingly in his ears, but Grandma was nowhere to be found; then MrJames realized he had been talking out loud to himself and he knew the knowledge, insight, and understanding related to these four portals and doorways must need be important.

Therefore, all readers and hearers; the words of chapter 11; see with your eyes, hear with your ears, perceive in your mind, receive in your heart. These four are entrance portals, and doorways of transfer of spiritual revelation, spiritual knowledge, spiritual insight, and spiritual understanding. However, skillful Godly wisdom only comes from the Most High God—Eternal Heavenly Father, Supreme Creator, Master Designer of all that exists.

Read this chapter in The Book of Proverbs yourself; in order to receive the messages this Proverb sends to you. Then, all readers and hearers, consider the question: will you make use of this knowledge, insights, and spiritual understanding to assist you in the art of living; to improve positive outcomes, and to reflect the blueprint of my divine purpose, as foreordained in the eternal realm of existence?

Finally, Grandma and MrJames believe all the Proverbs seem to be a reminder repeatedly that: The Sovereign Most High God—Our Eternal Heaven Father, Supreme Eternal Creator, and Master Designer of ALL that exists "directs our paths" and HE will lead us to become what we were destined to become. And, if we do all that we can do, trust that all things do work together so we will accomplish and fulfill the full measure of our divine created purpose.

Remember: He (or she) who knows and knows he (or she) knows is wise. He (or she) who knows and lives and conducts themselves according to what he (or she) knows is the wiser. However, he (or she) who knows but knows not that he knows is yet vulnerable, simple-minded, still unlearned, immature, ignorant, and foolish. Too soon old, and too late smart. So much the older, but unlike expensive wine and gourmet cheese; are you not getting any better?

Believe this ancient Proverb from the eternal realms, about the art of living: "Keep living like you are living, and you just get old, and older; then, you just die" and soon find out, that there is not a right way to do a wrong thing. Therefore, Stop —Pause; Listen--Attune; Observe—Do; Think—Reflect; Retain—Remember; skillful Godly wisdom is the roadway leading to prudence, providence and divine destiny.

There is no other way!

In the name of Jesus Christ. Amen.

13

DAY 12 - TRUST REVERENCE HUMILITY

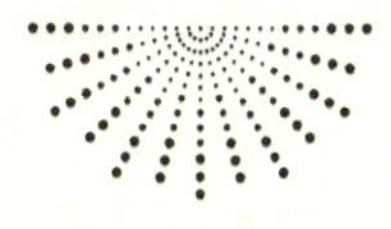

PROVERBS 12

Today is the twelfth consecutive day this month of reading a chapter each day from Proverbs, as a challenge issued by MrJames LifeCoach. Whosoever would, was welcomed to join him any day, but preferably every day to glean from his insights and impressions, personal thoughts, feedback, and comments. He continues his daily commitment to read the chapter from Proverbs each day that coincides with the date of the month; a process he has continued consistently now for five years.

Mostly, MrJames LifeCoach reads from the King James Version, but his insights and impressions are also based on readings in the New King James, New International, and Amplified Classic Version of the Holy Bible.

MrJames titled his challenge "The Art of Living" and describes it as persistent, unrelenting determination to continue pushing forward in life; no matter what life may throw in the way of your quest; and to become a reflection of the blueprint of your divinely created purpose for being here on this planet. His successful approach as a LifeCoach—also known as an accountability partner—is to first determine and establish whether a potential client is sincerely committed to a better way of living; guiding them in discovering and voluntarily making a commitment to focus and aim efforts and energy on the art of living their divinely created life purpose.

As a LifeCoach, MrJames assesses whether the new potential partner understands, believes in, accepts as truth, can explain the concept of a divinely created life purpose; and can relate the "concept" to their life.

The Art of Living requires individuals to consider, embrace, and internalize a spiritual life-view; and to accept the basic belief of the existence of a Supreme Eternal Creator—Sovereign God—Master Designer of all that exists.

Therefore, it stands up to reason that "everything happens [in this world of existence] for a reason" (cause and effect); in other words and from a spiritual perspective: "there is no such thing as an accident"—defined as an unforeseen, unintended, or an unexpected event.

As a LifeCoach, this is not just a core belief, it is the guidepost of absolute truth; it is the structure and foundation to the art of living; and it leads to acceptance; a unified agreement interconnecting present constructs of reality with invisible, celestial, and eternal realms.

A thought from MrJames LifeCoach on Proverbs 12:

MrJames LifeCoach belief in "nothing, absolutely nothing ever happening in this world by accident" was an insight he thought came to him through Grandma. However, while reading this chapter this time, the insight revealed itself, as if rising out from the abyss of the eternal realms, seemingly like Phoenix rising from the ashes, but entering into the understanding of MrJames through the words of this chapter of The Book of Proverbs.

Amazingly, while feeling a connection into the eternal realms, a feel-good, calm, relaxing, and peaceful sensation impacted the inner being of MrJames. He became consciously alert and aware that he had been thinking out loud, vocally expressive, but respectfully acknowledging that it was not Grandma.

Simultaneously, immediate and suddenly throughout every fiber of his being, MrJames knew absolutely that it was his commitment, consistency, continuous reading, and companionship study of the Scriptures and The Book of Wisdom—two or more (Matt 18:20), that has opened the doorway leading to the deepening of his insights and understandings on the art of living.

The root cause and essence of the art of living is the gaining of useful, skillful, and Godly wisdom from each of our daily experiences, our social interactions, all associations, verbal, and nonverbal communications. Nevertheless, and all too often, most of us will not begin to embrace a divinely created purpose for our life until later.

In the process and passing of time, it is then only when we come to acknowledge in the span of our lives we are getting "too soon old, too late smart" and our life chances are drifting away. This is the third back-to-back chapter continuing to make a comparison between the outcomes in the lives of the wicked, alongside outcomes in the lives of the righteous.

There is no other reasonable, rational, and sensible way to interpret the meaning from this chapter and the last two chapters as well; other than seeing the chapter as another comparison of righteous and wicked; good and evil. MrJames LifeCoach can now see Chapter 12 as a billowing, beckoning call to the wicked, with evidence- based moaning (vs 17-20), testimonials (vs 1-3), and firsthand from recorded, canonized, and also upside down, moral and immoral; and the up-down seesaw life of wise King Solomon.

The writers are sounding an alarm; and at least through these three chapters, the message is clear: wicked will not escape punishment and the righteous will always come out ahead in the long run.

Reading chapter twelve reminds MrJames LifeCoach that he was once a top student at A #1 Knucklehead University, but had finally graduated from the School of Hardknocks

Academy. Consequently, MrJames considers this Proverb as well; as the voice of Guardian Angels from the past; shining glimmers and flashing lights of knowledge to illuminate the steps on the pathway of your divinely created life.

Fittingly, it was previously said "knowledge is power," and the availability of that power, as implied in this chapter is in fact associated with skillful Godly wisdom; however—"she" must be desired, looked for, and pursued if we are to produce a life of divine purpose? Remember, wickedness can and never will bring real happiness; because seemingly, the life course has a built-in scale of balance.

In essence, you will reap what you sow (Gal 6:7-9); and ill-gotten gain will not pass the test of time and will not be profitable in the long-term. Remember readers and hearers, be ye mindful to remain fully focused on living in the divine purpose for your lives, and accept all life experiences as beneficial to that divine process.

Therefore, MrJames LifeCoach is encouraging each of you to read this Proverb for yourself, identify the meaningful instructions and receive the message this Proverb sends to you.

Finally, inclined to believe Grandma desires him to do so; MrJames reminds us all, over and over again you: God—Our Heavenly Father, Our Creator, Supreme Being, and Master Designer of all that exists "directs our paths" and will lead us to become what we were destined to become. And if we do all that we can do, trust that all things do work together so we will accomplish and fulfill our divine created purpose.

Remember: Too soon old, and too late smart. So much the older, but unlike expensive wine and gourmet cheese; are you not getting any better? Believe this ancient Proverb from the eternal realms, about the art of living: "Keep living like you are living, and you just get old, and older; then, you just die" and soon find out, that there is not a right way to do a wrong thing.

Therefore, Stop—Pause; Listen—Attune; Observe—Do; Think—Reflect; Retain—Remember; skillful Godly wisdom is the roadway leading to prudence, providence, and divine destiny. There is no other way! Remember F.R.O.G. and Fully Rely On God.

In the name of Jesus Christ. Amen.

14
DAY 13 - WORDS OF POWER

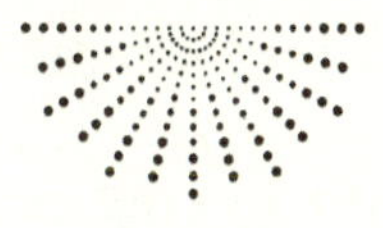

PROVERBS 13

Today is the thirteenth consecutive day of reading the chapter from Proverbs that coincides with that date of the month; as a challenge issued by MrJames LifeCoach. Whosoever was welcomed to join him daily to share their personal thoughts and feedback with him, as he keeps his daily commitment to read a chapter of Proverbs each day. MrJames LifeCoach has now engaged consistently in this process and continued doing so for five years.

MrJames LifeCoach has as an initial goal, as an effective accountability partner, to first access whether the potential client is sincerely ready; because he believes "when the student is ready" to live in divine purpose, "the teacher [of the art of living] will appear."

Moving forward from that point, he makes a formal assessment of whether the client understands, believes in, and can explain to the LifeCoach the concept of divine created purpose. Then he helps the client begin to identify what that purpose may be (vs 1,10).

The Art of Living requires individuals to consider and internalize a life-view that embraces and accepts a basic core belief of the existence of a Supreme, Most High, Eternal Creator—God—The Master Designer of all that exists.

As such and in essence, believing "everything happens for a reason" and there is no such thing as an accident. The crux and highpoint of the art of living is to gain useful, skillful, and Godly wisdom from each of our daily experiences, our social interactions, and our verbal and nonverbal communications (vs 2-3).

MrJames LifeCoach has a core foundational premise for clients; it is the absolute acceptance of all daily life experiences as: "it is what it is". This includes pleasant and not so pleasant; and the desired and undesired. More importantly, he guides clients, readers, and hearers of the words of Proverbs to accept earth-shaking and life-shattering experiences are tailor-made interactions with divine purpose, with meaning, and with a life-lesson laced and woven into the fabric of that real-life experience (vs 9,12).

Oftentimes, in the construct of reality, inspiration (TEACHER) only comes after we have come to that place in life where we begin to acknowledge, in the span of our life, we are getting "too soon old, too late smart;" and like water flowing under the bridge, our life chances are constantly drifting and gradually fading out and away (vs 14-16).

A thought from MrJames LifeCoach on Proverbs 13:

This chapter continues just as the last four have, making a comparison between different outcomes in the lives of the wicked alongside the righteous. Since this same focus is present through chapter 15, there is no way to interpret these consecutive chapters other than as an unmistakable beckoning, repeated call to the wicked, shouting out loudly with evidence-based testimony, and using the words of wise King Solomon himself.

MrJames LifeCoach accepts the words of chapter 13 as a repetitive soundbite coming through a megaphone; a crescendo of blaring warnings alerting the wicked that they will not escape their due punishment.

In contrast, King Solomon's words are predictively informing, prophesying positive outcomes to the righteous who avoid dishonesty, slothful mediocrity; and who walks in the ways of the wise, heeding "skillful godly wisdom."

The promise to the righteous who obey the counsel in this chapter is that they will come out ahead in the long run (vs 4,11,20-21). MrJames LifeCoach considers the entire Book of Proverbs to be like a beacon and beckoning voice from

Guardian Angels from the past; and from the blueprint of coming days; whispering into our present. This chapter, alongside the four previous ones; is shedding forth light and flashes of knowledge onto future days that are yet in front of us; and is illuminating the pathway of our foreordained divinely created life.

However, this chapter is a reminder for MrJames, who might just be talking to himself, because in past days he was that top student in A #1 Knucklehead University; but he did finally graduate from that School of Hardknocks.

The challenge he issued to whomsoever, asking them to read from The Book of Proverbs daily, was based on Alcoholics Anonymous ("AA") proverbial "one day at a time" approach to untangling the unmanageability of the art of living. MrJames shares lessons, insights, and understandings gained traveling his life course; testifies of skillful Godly wisdom he learned from reading The Book of Proverbs; and that paved his pathway leading to a better way of living.

Immediately, after recording the above statement, MrJames began to perceive in his conscious awareness, the inaudible but vibrational sound of the voice of Grandfather Richard; from behind the eyes and between the ears.

Grandfather Richard told MrJames: "YoungMan, remember and do not forget that these last four chapters became Grandfather's favorites. So, to the readers and hearers of these words, say thank you to them for standing-up, and for answering the challenge; but you must need to insist, persist, and plead to them that they follow the instructions and counsel—greater light and knowledge, that is being placed before them as they stay committed to the challenge."

Then, seemingly on the wings of a whisper, MrJames heard in his insides, in a sincere and solemn voice Grandfather said: "YoungMan, tell them that I can see from the eternal realms that many of them are just a stubborn KnuckleHead, just like I was before you were old enough to remember." Grandfather must have noticed shock on the face of MrJames as he continued to whisper: "Inez"— that is what he called her when he was expressing his affection towards Grandma—she promised me she would never tell you; YoungMan, about my Knuckle-headed-ness."

Unaware in his conscious mind, MrJames said out loud in an emotional outburst, but somehow, he was speaking directly into the very essence, fiber, and cell structure of Grandfather; when he said: But Grandfather how did you get her to do that?

Although invisible to his conscious presence, but undoubtedly conscious and aware of the question; Grandfather said in a distinct but inaudible voice: "That Woman!" He would addressed Grandma that way, only when Grandfather was about to do something she really wanted him to do.

However, although he had agreed to do it; he sounded just like Adam in the Garden of Eden (Genesis 3:12), and Jesus

Christ in the Garden of Gethsemane (Matt 26:39); if he had it his way he really might not do it. Then, I felt the intense vibration of these love filled, Earth-shaking, and mountain-moving words come across his tongue, thru his lips, and out of his mouth. Grandfather. said: YoungMan, I promised! Inez; that someday I would tell you this myself; but not knowing at that time that I would be doing it from the eternal realm of my existence."

As grandfather continued in speaking to MrJames, the vibration of his voice was beginning to fade: "Tell readers and hearers that following the counsel of the Proverbs on a daily basis, will lead to improved outcomes in the art of living, and keep them focused on the eternal blueprint of a divinely created purpose…….(Total silence)….Grandfather was gone……

Fittingly, through the words of Proverbs and even from eternal realms, we are warned and forewarned that wickedness will not bring the happiness we crave and seek; ill-gotten gain will not be sustained and will not be profitable to us in the long-term.

Remember, the intent of a LifeCoach is to hold individuals accountable to themselves; introduce them to a better and more beneficial way to live; and to encourage individuals to accept all real-life experiences as being helpful, to a divine process that was thought-out beforehand, on the blueprint of the days of their lives.

MrJames LifeCoach continues to encourage those who accepted the challenge to read this chapter of Proverb for yourself; to identify meaningful repeated instructions; and to receive the messages this Proverb sends.

These beginning chapters of The Book of Proverbs, remind MrJames of "10 Absolute Core Life Beliefs" he primarily gleaned from exposure, reading, in- depth studying of The Book of Wisdom; and from his more than six decades in art of living through real-life earth- shaking and earth-shattering experiences.

Finally, applying his belief in the benefits of repetition, MrJames LifeCoach reminds us again: God—Our Heavenly Father, Our Creator, Supreme Being, and Master Designer of all that exists "directs our paths" and will lead us to become what we were destined to become. And, when we do all that we can do, trust that all things will and do work together so we accomplish and fulfill our divine created purpose.

Remember: He who knows and knows he knows is wise. However, he who knows but knows not that he knows is yet still unlearned, immature, and ignorant. Therefore, Stop—pause; Listen—tune-in; Observe—just do it; Think—meditate and reflect; Retain—recall and remember; these are guideposts on the roadway leading to prudence, providence and divine destiny.

Believe this ancient Proverb from the eternal realms of Grandmas and Grandfathers; as divine instructions relating to the art of living: "Keep living like you are living, and you just get old; older, and older; but not the wiser. Then, after the days are gone, you just die (Ecc 9:3); but soon realize that there is not; was not; and there never will be a right way to do a wrong thing.

In the name of Jesus Christ. Amen.

15

DAY 14 - THE LYING TONGUE

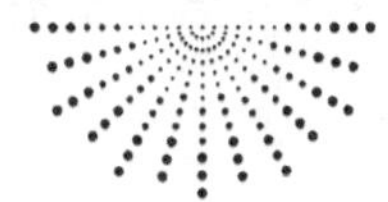

PROVERBS 14

Today is the fourteenth consecutive day—two weeks of reading a different chapter from The Book of Proverbs each day as a challenge issued by MrJames, LifeCoach. Whosoever desired to do so was welcomed to join him in his daily quest and commitment to read the chapter from Proverbs that coincides with the date of the month.

MrJames, LifeCoach, has consistently continued this pattern for five years, and traditionally he reads from the King James Version. Remember, thoughts, insights, and impressions will be based on wording from reading New King James, New International, New Living Translation, and the Amplified Classic Version of the Holy Bible.

MrJames' success as a LifeCoach—accountability partner he attributes to his initial aim and primary focus to identify and only accept potential clients sincerely ready to diligently seek after and discover the divine purpose of their life. MrJames knows from personal real-life experiences: "when the student is ready" to live in divine purpose, "the teacher will always appear." With confirmation and affirmation from the prospect, he then administers a formal assessment to determine whether the client understands, believes in, and can briefly explain to LifeCoach the concept of divinely created purpose.

Moving forward from that point; in agreement and partnership with the client, they begin to identify and discover the unique divinely created purpose of their life. Therefore, based on that foundational belief, MrJames, LifeCoach, asserts: "everything happens for a reason and there is no such thing as a true and independent accident." Consequentially, the Sovereign, Supreme, Eternal Creator—God—Master Designer of all that exists is always in control of all things (James 1:1-8).

The essence of the art of living is to gain, apply, or opportunities to use skillful Godly wisdom in each daily experience, social interaction; both verbal and nonverbal communications, and from our individual thoughts and impressions (vs 15-19).

Nonetheless, all too often, many of us will not begin to embrace the divinely created purpose for life until later-on in the life-course span; and oftentimes it is only after tragedy, trauma, or an unforeseen or unintended incident occurs. Thus, it is then that we come to acknowledge on the life journey that in our span of life we are truly getting "too soon old, too late smart" and our life chances are constantly slowly drifting away.

The proverbial clock on the wall continuously goes: Tic tock, tic tock; but never stops.

A thought from MrJames LifeCoach on Proverbs 14:

This chapter continues making comparison between different outcomes in the lives of the prideful, foolish, and wicked; alongside the prudent, wise, and righteous. MrJames makes it known to those who answered the challenge and continues committed; that this comparison will be prevalent and present through chapter 15; but subtle and indirectly referenced through each chapter.

There is no doubt in the interpretation of the last five consecutive chapters (10-14); a beckoning call to the wicked; a constant repetitive utterance stated distinctly clear, blasting out warnings to the wicked— These are they who are "fully ripe in iniquity" (2 Ne 28:16), whose thoughts are evil continually (Genesis 6:5); spiritually blinded; unable to see the feared disaster that is looming (Prov 101:24), if they continue the path they are choosing to travel.

The perceived voice, sounding like Grandma and Grandfather Richard; echoing out of this chapter it sounds like MrJames is thinking out loud and talking to himself again.

However, he hears no audible sound; he feels the essence of

skillful Godly wisdom; speaking from the perspective of someone who has looked into the future. This explains exactly how MrJames feels about constant daily reading the Proverbs.

Grandma said these very words to MrJames one day: "Baby, constant daily reading in the scriptures" is like having an art of living GPS; or looking into a "Liahona—crystal ball—compass or director" (Alma 37:38); especially when you voluntarily invest time reading The Book of Proverbs.

Grandma and Grandfather Richard believed; it was because an influence from eternal realms mixes with our "simple-minded human understanding" by painting a picture on the screen of our minds that expands our perceptions as we read the words.MrJames believes, from reading Sacred Scriptures and from his constant reading of Proverbs; that a central message in all Scriptures describes a comparative futuristic perspective of what life will look like for the wicked juxtaposed against the righteous; when they both reach their earned—"wages of sin is death;" or their appointed—"gift of God is eternal life" (Rom 6:23). And the juxtaposition of their final destiny based on lived standards and principles of the art of living.

While reading and reflecting on these chapters MrJames, LifeCoach, remembers being "stuck on stupid" in a past life and sitting at the head of his class at A #1 Knucklehead University. It is verse 14 that reminds him of his gratitude for finally taking heed to "skillful Godly wisdom" and graduating from the School of Hardknocks Academy.

Repeatedly, MrJames LifeCoach shares valuable lessons he had the privilege to learn; lessons that now serve as a pathway to a better way of living life, that leads to improved outcomes in the art of living; and serves to keep him traveling between the white lines and guideposts of his divinely created life purpose.

Moving on from that point, after reading Proverbs or any Scriptures, since "all scriptures are profitable and beneficial to readers (2 Tim 3:16-17), both believers and non-believers; then decide for yourself how you will apply the skillful Godly wisdom and insights into your daily construction, and trials related to the art of living on divine purpose.

Believe this ancient Proverb from the eternal realms, about the art of living: "Keep living like you are living, and you just get old, and older; then, you just die" and soon find out, the absolute truth, that there is not, was not, and never will be a right way to do a wrong thing .

In the name of Jesus Christ. Amen.

16
POWERLESSNESS AND UNMANAGEABILITY

WEEK TWO

As MrJames concludes the second week, immediately in his mind he begins thinking about the start of week three. He began to recognize he was feeling an absence of direction; and subconsciously he believes he was waiting for the influence of Grandma, Grandfather, or any of his Guardian Angels to appear. Total and complete silence continued…

MrJames, growing a bit impatient, decides to read from his King James Version Holy Bible. No sooner than he had picked it up, he began hearing vaguely and detecting a faint whisper that was hard to distinguish. Sitting quiet as a mouse, and still holding onto his Holy Bible, but he had not opened it yet; he continued attempting to tune in to the voice. Suddenly, although MrJames had not noticed it was even on and running; the air-conditioning cycled off; and as it came to pass within a second or two in the passing moment; the refrigerator also cycled off.

Oddly enough, MrJames had noticed neither had been on and in full cycle. The extreme silence triggered a funny thought and memory of Grandma in the mind of MrJames, that made him chuckle out loud. Then with a wide smile on his face he said: "Grandma, it's so quiet you could hear a rat piss on cotton in here" and as the words left his mouth, the hard-to-detect voice became clear and distinct.

Still feeling a sense of loss for direction and not knowing what to do, but wanting to continue to move forward reading Proverbs, He heard the vague and fading voice saying: "YoungMan, I am Teacher" and MrJames remembered Grandma had told him, when the student was ready the Teacher would appear. Although he did not ask the question that was on his mind; Teacher answered it; he said in the mind of MrJames: "Baby, yes; I am he; and you are the student; and it has been observed from the eternal realms that you are indeed ready" and waiting with your Bible in hand." (Total Silence)

Feeling doubtful, uncertain, and inadequate MrJames said to himself: "I wonder who decided I was ready? Who decided I ever wanted to be a student? What happened to Grandma? Why is it so quiet in here...

Question after question, after question filled the mind of MrJames.

Then, somehow through the silence and from the eternal realms, where Guardian Angels: Grandparents, Ancient Ancestors, and the other Guardian Angels we may have encountered now reside. Teacher made his presence known to MrJames. Holding onto his Bible a bit tighter, he heard Teacher say his name: "MrJames LifeCoach, it is the foreordained time for you to gain deeper insights into the art of living; and time to reinforce and solidify other eternal absolute truths and principles, relating to living a better life; and reaping the more desired positive outcomes." Giving no time for a response from MrJames, there it was again... (Total silence, again)...

Breaking through the silence once more, Teacher asked MrJames this haunting question: "MrJames, what do you do when you don't know what to do" and the silence returned...

Feeling somewhat defeated, disappointed, and discouraged; MrJames unclutched his hand holding his Bible and laid it on the table. As he Did so, the pages opened and MrJames saw these words on the screen of his mind; and just as he saw that there were words in his head, he noticed that his Bible had opened to James Chapter I when it opened on its own...

Powerless & Unmanageable
1st Person Singular:

I am a unique, wonderful, and precious child of the Most High God. Put here on this earth for a preordained purpose; to love, adore, and appreciate my life on the earth plane of physical existence; and the art of living experience.

Life, even with all its twists and turns; it has been, it is now, and will continue unfolding undoubtedly just as planned by

God—Supreme Creator—Heavenly Father—Master Designer of Heaven, Earth and all that exists. I recognize that all my life experiences have "worked together" to make me who I am today. Therefore, without regrets and with content acceptance, from behind my eyes and between my ears, I willingly surrender and submit my right of refusal of any life experience, in exchange for "consecrated afflictions" (2 Nephi 1:1-2) and trials.

Despite it all, I express gratitude to God; and I am eternally grateful to the art of living and for the existence of a divine blueprint of my life journey. I once was a blinded Knucklehead, but now I can see clearly; if any facet of my life were left out, altered, or changed in any manner; I would not be who I am today.

I like myself, I like myself, I like myself (an excellent mantra to repeat daily). I am a good person and thankful to God things are as well as they are.

Not just for today, but everyday I remind myself that I am a child of the most high God; that I was formed by the Creator of Heaven and Earth; and there is a great purpose which only I can fulfill. Lucifer –the Devil—Satan—the accusing adversary of Mankind; *"like"* a roaring lion he is going about (really, He is just a declawed pussycat), "seeking whom he may devour" (1 Peter 5:8), and it is my prayer that I be not entangled and counted amongst his captives again.

Therefore, moving forward, I desire divine guidance, divine intervention, divine revelation, spiritual knowledge, inspiration and enlightenment, and skillful Godly wisdom and insights in the art of living in this present dispensation and the fullness of time. I desire only: to be, to say, to do; and to become that unto which I was created to become.

As I contemplate trails and the trials ahead; and ponder their meaning; I know the Guardian Angels: Surely, Goodness, and Mercy shall follow me all the days of my life (Psalms 23:6). I pray through the righteousness of Christ—(worthiness), and fervency—(favor) of a child making my request known to the Father—(inheritance), asking that guardian angels overtake me, hedge up the way around me—(divine protection); and that I may not offend God the Eternal Father (eternal friendship and fellowship). How grateful I am for the blessings of life and for the knowledge of the Lord, as my personal Savior, even I know him as Jesus The Christ.

I ask forgiveness first for my willfully committed sin, my sins of omission—failure to do, my sins due to imperfections and shortcomings; may my human weakness (Ether 12:27) not be a hindrance unto those around me; and that I am no longer blinded by the cunning deceit of the enemy. Father, may I ever be mindful that this world is eternally controlled by the laws of "cause & effect." I acknowledge that human emotions are consequential and difficult to master and control; especially those that are deeply rooted in the incidents and circumstances of the past.

It is my experience that the way to be released from the grips of the negative influences of the past are: 1. Acknowledge their existence. 2. Admit personal "Powerlessness and Unmanageability" over the effects; 3. Yield to Sovereign God—controls all—all things work together for good (lovers of God and called of God) Father, I realize that nothing is neither fortunate or unfortunate as I travel the highways of my life; it is my perspective from behind me eyes and between my ears that gives meaning to happenings in my life; and I admit the existence of present emotional struggle relating to matters in my distant past. Nevertheless, I desire only to do that which is right; and I understand that there is in fact not a right way to do a WRONG thing. Furthermore, it is my desire to be an instrument in the hands of God for righteousness—in good standing; always in the good, acceptable, and perfect will of God.

Therefore, again, I come boldly to the throne of grace (Heb 4:16), seeking skillful Godly wisdom from heaven; that further light, knowledge, and understanding may be forthcoming pertaining to current life-challenging issues; and consequences hovering over me from a past riddled with errors in my choices and judgment. I await the Spirit of the Lord, as a still quiet voice, to come unto me and "renew a right spirit unto me" (Psalm 51:10-12); and I ask forgiveness for any impure thoughts, actions, and ill-intent; that it be removed from me as I seek the constant companionship of the Holy Ghost.

In the name of Jesus Christ. Amen.

17

DAY 15 - IDLENESS AND PROCRASTINATION

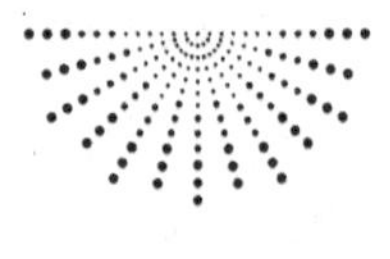

PROVERBS 15

Starting off the day reading James 1:2-8; MrJames acknowledges today is the fifteenth consecutive day this month reading a different chapter from The Book of Proverbs. This challenge, issued by MrJames LifeCoach, is a way for whomsoever to make an investment in their individual self-pursuit of wisdom; by choosing any day, every day, or just one day to expose oneself to The Book of Wisdom.

Join MrJames in his daily commitment to read the chapter of Proverbs each day that coincides with that date of the month; a process MrJames LifeCoach has been engaged in and doing consistently for nearly five years. Respectfully, he regards King James Version as his standard text, his insights and reflections are based on reading from New King James, New International, New Living Translation; and Amplified Classic Version of the Holy Bible.

MrJames knows from real-life experience that "when the student is ready" to live in individual and divine purpose: "the teacher will appear." From that baseline of experiences, he helps the client begin to explore and discover the unique and divinely created purpose of their life; and identify potential pitfalls that distract them from that purpose.

MrJames explains: "the Art of Living on purpose requires that each individual consider, embrace, and internalize a life-view that accepts a basic core belief of the existence of a Supreme Eternal Creator—God—Master Designer of all that exists."

From that baseline of accepted foundational belief: "it follows that everything happens for a reason; and there is no such thing as a true accident—unforeseen, unintended, and unexpected events; because the Sovereign Supreme Eternal Creator—God—Master Designer of all that exists is always in control of ALL things.

MrJames uses basic absolute core beliefs, as a foundational premise to the art of living and the acceptance of all life experiences; this includes the pleasant, the not so pleasant, and especially the life-shaking and life-shattering ones.

In the construct of spiritual reality and on the physical Earth plane, all experiences are tailor-made with a divine purpose, a divine meaning, and valuable life lessons interwoven into the experience.

The essence of the art of living is for the gaining of useful, skillful Godly wisdom from each of our daily life experiences, our social interactions, verbal and nonverbal communications, our thoughts, spiritual insights, mental perceptions, and revelatory impressions.

Remember, oftentimes for most of us it is only after tragedy that we come to acknowledge on the life journey, and late in the span of life when we become consciously aware that we are getting “too soon old, too late smart” and our life chances for successful living are gradually drifting away. Abraham got up "early in the morning" (Gen 22:3); as my brother Karl would say: "to handle his business" and to get on his way to obey God. And what God had asked Abraham to do was A HARD THING! Yes.

My 20/20 "hindsight review" I must admit; during my knucklehead years, I may have managed to pull myself to get up; and may have even got on the way to obey by the "end" of the day; but that is, only if I obeyed at all. Quick and prompt to obey what I thought was some hard instructions from God is not reflected in the footprints in the sands of my life. Too soon old? Or, just too late smart! Abraham was old but he was also smart, and he was blessed for promptly doing what God had instructed, and so will we.

Therefore, I realize promptness in obedience brings forth blessings from Heavenly realms; and delayed obedience is akin to disobedience. Lord bless me and all readers that I might be swift to listen and hear your word, and prompt to obey and be a doer of the things that thou will command.

A thought from MrJames LifeCoach on Proverbs 15:

This is the ending chapter boldly illuminating the difference in outcomes in the lives of the wicked in contrast to the righteous; however, to a lesser degree, this comparison continues all through the remaining chapters as well. However, the beckoning repetitive warning in chapter 15th becomes a quieting crescendo, replaced by calling attention to the "mouth..., tongue..., lips..., thoughts..., heart..., attitude..., integrity..., the nature of the words we speak; and unspoken intentions and dispositions of the heart.

The voice of chapter 15 urges the use of skillful godly wisdom in the art of living. That message is communicated, using no uncertain terms, distinctly clear and as a billowing warning to avoid many real-life pitfalls by keeping a guard on our mouth.

The message painted in the words of the first few verses in the chapter describe desired traits of character necessary to begin to master the art of living. For example; traits and characteristics such as discipline, respect, joy, and goodness are prerequisites to living a purposeful and divinely created life.

MrJames is reminded, in this chapter, about personal real-life experiences from which he learned skillful godly wisdom, in the art of living; experience is the best teacher, but he believes personal experience can also be costly and most expensive; and sometime personal experience can be the most consequential way to learn, especially when learning from experiences of others has been made available to us.

Therefore, MrJames uses his firsthand experiences; absolute truths; and skillful Godly wisdom to blaze a pathway that leads readers to divine purpose and more positive outcomes in the art of living. LifeCoach remind the readers that "knowledge is power" and our words, thoughts, daily conduct, and how we apply the acquired knowledge is relevant and significant in determining the availability of that power.

Initial exposure to The Book of Proverbs by MrJames was hearing and seeing the principles active in the lives of his grandparents; after more than six decades in the art of living now, he was 12 years old when he completed reading the 31 chapters for the first time.

Moving forward in the process of time, after many real-life experiences in the art of living, the insights MrJames gained from skillful Godly wisdom of the Proverbs has become "10 Absolute Core Beliefs" and eternal truths for living a divinely created life on purpose.

I continue to encourage each of you to read Proverbs yourself, identify pertinent and especially repeated instructions; this positions readers to receive the spiritual insights, messages and meanings Proverbs can reveal. After reading The Book of Proverbs, you decide for yourself how you will apply wisdom from Proverbs to your life.

Finally, MrJames remind readers again: God—Our Heavenly Father, Our Creator, Sovereign Supreme Being, and Master Designer of all that exists "directs our paths" and will lead us to become what we were destined to become.

However, if we are not slothful, foolish, greedy for gain; and if we do all that we can do, fully trusting all things to work together (Rom 8:28), then we will accomplish and fulfill our divinely created purpose.

Remember: He (or she) who knows and knows he (or she) knows is wise. He (or she) who knows and lives and conducts themselves according to what he (or she) knows is the wiser. Too soon old, and too late smart. So much the older, but unlike expensive wine and gourmet cheese; are you not getting any better?

Choose ye this 15th day to believe this ancient Proverb from the eternal realms, about the art of living: "Keep living like you are living, and you just get old, and older; then, you just die" (Ecc. 9:3) and soon find out, that there is not a right way to do a wrong thing. Godly wisdom is the paved roadway leading to prudence, providence, and divine destiny. You be the judge! There is no other way!

In the name of Jesus Christ, amen.

18
DAY 16 - WORKS OF THE FLESH

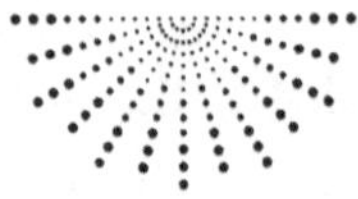

PROVERBS 16

Today is the sixteenth consecutive day reading a different chapter from Proverbs. The challenge was issued by MrJames LifeCoach; urging readers to make an investment in themselves and their pursuit of wisdom by accepting his daily commitment to read the chapter of Proverbs each day that coincides with the date of the month; a process he has continued now for five years.

Usually, as has been mentioned, he prefers reading the King James Version, but MrJames is reading from the New King James, New International, New Living Translation, and the Amplified Classic Version Holy Bible as a basis for his shared insights and understanding.

MrJames LifeCoach describes "The Art of Living" as persistent determination and continuation to push forward in your life quest to become what you were created to become, no matter what life may throw at you along the way.

He has learned from his real-life experiences that "when the student is ready" to live in divine purpose, "the TEACHER will appear" and the art of living will require individuals to ponder, consider, embrace, and internalize a life-view that accepts a basic core belief of the existence of a Supreme Eternal Creator—God—Master Designer of ALL that exists.

Therefore, from that foundational belief, everything happens for a reason, and there is no such thing as an accident, a core belief that is also implied and expressed in verse 33 of this chapter. A Sovereign—Most High God—Supreme Creator—Eternal Father—Master Designer of all that exists is always in control of ALL things.

MrJames uses other basic absolute core beliefs to help facilitate acceptance of all life experiences as tailor-made and divinely appointed. This includes the pleasant, the not so pleasant, and especially life-shaking and life-shattering challenges, tests, tribulations, and trials; ALL experiences are specially ordered with divine purpose, divine meaning, and valuable life lessons interwoven into the experience. Real-life experiences have the uncanny ability to serve as effective tutors in the art of living out our divinely created purpose.

See Jonah 1-4; Jonah, on the other hand and from a differing perspective; was not like Abraham when instructed by God to do something Jonah did not want to do. On this occasion, it was not necessarily because it was such a hard thing for Jonah to do; Jonah just did not want to do the thing.

Therefore, Jonah goes off in the opposite direction attempting to run away from what God has for him, and only him, to do. Now, think about it; how foolish is that; if God is omniscient—ALL KNOWING, knows all things from beginning to end; omnipresent—ALWAYS in the Present, Here, There, Everywhere; how do we run and hide from God?

My personal experience have tutored me to know that that does not work out to be pleasant; and from my 20/20 hind sighted Knucklehead perspective; and a quick review of the footprints in the sands of my life; I can see a mirror reflection of Jonah; and it looks like we are sitting side by side; self-medicating, trying to comfort ourselves through the misery of our rebellion and stubbornness.

As I ponder this thought, together with reading this chapter; I am thinking out loud to myself saying: "To thine own-self be true" and asking myself this question: "Am I still just a Knucklehead in the belly of a big fish (whale)? And whatever my life-controlling issue may be, is it because I have been running from something God has for me, and only me, to do?

Yes, yes, yes; MrJames believes many of us should answer in the affirmative. Jonah is now willing to obey, but being brought to this point of willingness, Jonah finds himself in a certain place (circumstance or situation).

Readers, did you answer the challenge after finding yourself in a certain place? Are you now anxiously awaiting to be spit back up, so you can promptly go handle the business of God? Are you feeling like a tightly twisted toy soldier, coiled-up and ready to take off speeding down that path? Have you "come to yourself" (Luke 15:17)? In the art of living, are you feeling excited, impatient, and anxious as a little child waiting for Christmas morning? To thine own-self be true!

Reading through the Proverbs consistently has allowed MrJames to sneak a peek into the room; he has already seen all the toys that are awaiting you. Therefore, I can hardly wait for you to live to reflect the blueprint of your divinely created purpose.

Furthermore, now I realize that running from God truly just brings F.R.O.G.S. into your life: Frustration; Rejection; Opposition; Grievances; and Sinful acts. Sometimes they show up in the form of a big fish. Bless all of your children, Heavenly Father, with an increased desire to do those things that thou created each of us to do.

Nevertheless, oftentimes most of us will still not begin to embrace the divinely created purpose for our life until later on in the life-course span of time. All too often, for many of us, it is only after a tragedy, or a seemingly unfortunate incident on our life journey that we come to acknowledge, in our span of life, we are getting "too soon old, too late smart" and our timetable of life chances is gradually being depleted and drifting away beyond our reach.

A thought from MrJames LifeCoach on Proverbs 16:

A familiar verse in this chapter establishes this eternal standard: "pride goes before destruction and a haughty spirit goes before a fall". In other words, think of it this way, "birds of a feather flock together." Therefore; following alongside, behind, or in the wake of a "prideful and haughty spirit" will undoubtedly reside shame, embarrassment, and disaster.

This chapter further highlights the effectual power of not just the words we speak but the attitude, feelings, emotions, and the disposition that accompany the words we speak. Moving forward through Proverbs there is repetitive mention of the "mouth…, tongue…, lips…, heart…, thoughts…, attitude…, and integrity—sincere honesty. MrJames, LifeCoach, notes this Proverb adds more comparisons of outcomes and expectations of the wicked, measured against the righteous.

In this chapter, MrJames notes in honor of Guardian Angel Deemyrron; Solomon uses a maximum- sized amplified Bluetooth Speaker megaphone, mounted atop a proverbial "rooftop" to stress an even greater emphasis on the importance and seriousness to his words.

This chapter announces with absolute certainty that the Supreme Creator—God—Master Designer of all that exist, not only knows our thoughts, but He also knows "the motives behind our thoughts" (vs1-3).

However, as our heart and mind align with the will of our divinely created life purpose, our thoughts will begin to be conducive to successful outcomes, increased understanding, and will guide us to live in our divinely created purpose.

The voice of the chapter continues to urge the pursuit to gain skillful Godly wisdom in the art of living; and the message is repeated and communicated using no complex uncertain terms.

Moreover, there is a distinct, clear, and billowing warning that if heeded we avoid many life pitfalls, primarily by keeping a guard on the words of our mouth.

Furthermore, the message painted by the chosen words of this chapter describe additional traits and character components necessary for improvement in art of living outcomes.

Our Godly actions, reactions, conduct, and behaviors; as well as our natural tendencies and traits; and characteristics such as discipline, respect, discretion, and goodness are prerequisites and must need be established as standard guiding principles when living a purposeful and divinely created life. Remember, all of life's experiences can be beneficial to the divine process.

The Initial insights that Twelve-year-old MrJames received nearly six decades ago and after many real-life experiences in the art of living; has become "10 Absolute Core Beliefs" of his life. MrJames, LifeCoach, claims that they are eternal truths specifically from The Book of Proverbs, Holy Bible; and other Sacred Scriptures and writings; upon which to build and live a purpose-filled divinely created life.

Thus, MrJames encourages each of you to read Proverbs yourself, for the purpose of specifically identifying pertinent repeated instructions; for the gaining of deeper insights; for revealed spiritual understanding; and for more positive outcome in the art of living as a return on your investing time in reading the Proverbs.

He (she) who Thinks
He (she) Knows, But Really Knows not;
Is yet Ignorant, Foolish, Immature, and Unlearned;
He (she) Can be a Nuisance, And Can Drive Away HIM who is Wiser; And, Can Even Quench The Holy Spirit

Remember and believe this ancient Proverb from the eternal realms, about the art of living: "Keep living like you are living, and you just get old, and older; then, you just die" (Ecc. 9:3) and soon find out, that there is not a right way to do a wrong thing.

Therefore, Stop—pause; Listen—tune-in; Observe—just do it; Think—reflect; and Retain—remember; applying skillful Godly wisdom is the roadway leading to prudence, providence, and divine destiny. There is no other way!

In the name of Jesus Christ, amen.

19
DAY 17 - ABSOLUTE TRUTHS

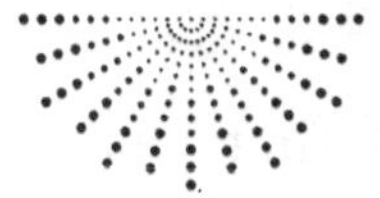

PROVERBS 17

Today is the seventeenth consecutive day this month for those who answered the challenge on the first day, reading a different chapter from Proverbs. This challenge, titled "The Art of Living," was issued by MrJames LifeCoach. He asked readers to make an investment in themselves and their pursuit to obtain skillful Godly wisdom by committing to read daily from Proverbs—The Book of Wisdom.

Now, representing five years and counting, he has consistently continued daily reading the chapter of Proverbs that coincides with the date of the month. Read, ponder, reflect, review, and glean thoughts, personal impressions, and insights from his quest to obtain skillful Godly wisdom for the art of living journey.

Moving forward, MrJames will disclose and describe how the Art of Living requires each individual person to ponder, consider, embrace, and internalize a life-view that accepts a basic core belief of the existence of a Supreme Eternal Creator—God—Master Designer of all that exists. Building on the structure and foundation of this self-proclaimed absolute truth, all daily life experiences are tailor-made with divine purpose, divine meaning, and valuable life lessons interwoven into the experience.

Further insights reveal that real-life experiences have an uncanny ability to specifically serve as effective tutors in the art of living a divinely created purpose. Eventually, we come to accept "there is not a right way to do a wrong thing" but all too often, it is only after some perceived unfortunate mishap or tragedy.

Ultimately, we must need to begin to acknowledge that we are getting "too soon old, too late smart" and the timetable of our life span, and the content and quality of life chances are being gradually depleted and drifting away, like sands through the hourglass.

A thought from MrJames LifeCoach on Proverbs 17:

MrJames has recognized a familiar verse recorded in this chapter establishes eternal standards of joy, peace, happiness, cheerfulness, knowledge, and understanding as qualities, traits, and characteristics; in the art of living, that are to be desired, pursued, nourished, cultivated, and embraced. MrJames has found these attitudes, dispositions, and desires serve the inner being in a positive manner; and the contrasting opposite behaviors and conduct produce negative outcomes. MrJames LifeCoach recognizes that this Proverb adds more comparisons of outcomes; fruit, and harvest readers can predict to follow the wicked, liars, mockers, and scoffers—those who ridicule.

The Most High God—Master Designer of all that exists knows our thoughts and motives; and HE sees our insincere acts of ransom and bribery as pitfalls, potholes, and speed bumps in our divine pathway and serve to hinder positive progression in the art of living.

However, as our hearts and minds align with the will and blueprint of our divinely created purpose; and MrJames believes answering this challenge expedites the process, our thoughts will be conducive—helpful and will produce desired successful outcomes, increased understanding, and a closer adherence to living out the blueprint of our divinely created purpose.

The voice of chapter 17 continues to urge readers to pursue skillful godly wisdom in the art of living; a message that is repeatedly communicated in no uncertain terms, distinctly clear, and as a billowing warning to avoid many life pitfalls by keeping a guard on our mouth.

MrJames has learned from his six-and-half decades of living that it is best sometimes; especially when in the heat of passion and in human emotions, to remain silent rather than to be quick to speak; showing forth contempt—disrespect, immaturity—childish foolishness, and ignorance—naive and lacking of knowledge.

Furthermore, the picture message painted by the words of chapter 17 subtly describe conduct, behaviors, traits, and characteristics that follow as rewards for righteous; and consequences for actions categorized and labeled as transgression and dishonesty. His more than six decades of real-life experiences, persuades MrJames to remind readers that knowledge is power; but our words and speech, thoughts, daily conduct, and how we apply knowledge and acquired skillful Godly wisdom is significant in the art of living outcomes.

Suddenly, and without warning, an inaudible voice and the perceived presence of Teacher began to be housed in the conscious awareness of MrJames. While under the influence of HIS presence, MrJames was told: "MrJames, it was I who delivered the primitive insights to twelve-year- old MrJames. Teacher continued to explain to me behind my eyes and between my ears: "Only because YoungMan voluntarily obeyed the counsel from Grandma; and completed reading The Book of Proverbs the first time; and that was nearly six decades ago.

Now YoungMan has become MrJames; and after your many real-life experiences in the art of living, those early delivered insights and principles have become "10 Absolute Core Beliefs" of MrJames. Your acceptance of those insights, principles, and core beliefs led you to honor, recognize, and accept the insights, principles, standards, and the skillful

Godly wisdom of Proverbs, as eternal truths upon which to build a life to duplicate and reflect the blueprint of your divine purpose."

Unexpectedly, through HIS inaudible voice, Teacher said: 'MrJames, continue to encourage readers to read the Proverbs for themselves; with the intent to identify specific and pertinent insights for developing and constructing the art of living portrait of their lives." Then, to the surprise of MrJames, Teacher repeated the delivered message and instructions to MrJames exactly, word for word.

Except, as the perceived presence of Teacher began to decrease, and HIS voice became less pronounced and distinct; these words from Teacher came onto the mind-screen behind the eyes and between the ears of MrJames: "Proverbs will speak a ***profound message of revelation knowledge to each reader; and it shall come to pass, in process of time, Proverbs will speak, teach, and inspire each committed reader in a uniquely personal manner"***...(in came total silence)...Teacher was gone.

Finally, as always, coming to the end of another chapter, MrJames also reminds readers: Sovereign Most High God—Our Heavenly Father, Supreme Creator, and Master Designer of all that exists "directs our paths" and will lead us to become what we are destined to become; if we do all that we can do, trusting in HIM to do the rest; we are promised: "HIS grace is sufficient.

Remember: Knowledge is power. He who knows and knows he knows is wise. He who knows, lives, conducts himself, and does according to that which he knows is the wiser. However, he who knows but knows not that he knows is yet still unlearned, immature, and ignorant.

Therefore, Stop—pause; Listen— tune-in; Observe—just do it; Think—reflect; Retain—remember F.R.O.G.—Fully Rely On God; applying skillful Godly wisdom in the art of living is the roadway leading to prudence, providence, and divine destiny. There is no other way! This is the roadway to providence, and divine destiny.

In the name of Jesus Christ. Amen.

Coming Together Is: Important

Staying Together Is:

Progress

BUT

Working Together Is:

Success.

20
DAY 18 - AVOID THE FOOLISH

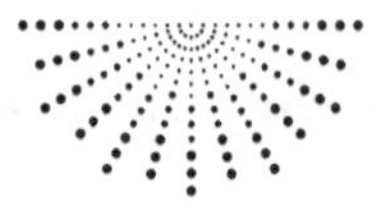

PROVERBS 18

MrJames is saying to readers, eighteen days into reading the corresponding chapter from Proverbs that coincides with that date of the month: "I know I might just be talking to myself today. I have come to understand, more often than not, in The Book of Wisdom and throughout the Holy Bible and other sacred Scriptures, the word we have translated into our English word 'heart' is not referring to the physical organ and muscle in the center of our chest cavity, keeping us alive, pumping and circulating life-sustaining blood (Lev 17:11-14) through the body.

However, that was the picture likely to be seen and perceived on the screen in my mind. Insights from reading Proverbs has MrJames translating the word 'heart' other ways. For example, it could be that 'heart' is a reference to the essence and nature of an individual. As such, the word may be better understood similar to the implied meaning of the phrase

'heart of a watermelon' that refers to the purest, sweetest part of that fruit.

Therefore, from that interpretation, the use of the word ***'heart'*** in the context of Scriptures, and in the Proverb; could be understood as a reference to: ***the inner core and pure sweetness, or in some cases the absolute sheer bitterness of the person.***

This perspective calls into attention the words of Master Teacher: ***'of the abundance of the 'heart' the mouth speaks'.*** Therefore, MrJames believes it is from the depth of the core essence of our convictions, thoughts, beliefs, and actions that our mouth speaks words from the core essence of our being.

Therefore, two shall become one is the result of the blending together of the core essence of two lives (hearts) is appropriately depicted and fittingly described as 'LOVE.' Moving forward from this point, as always, MrJames reads from the King James Version; but his shared insights are also based on his reading from the New King James; New International; New Living Translation; and Amplified Classic Versions of the Holy Bible.

Readers—as students engaged in reading and study of Sacred Scriptures, including The Book of Proverbs; you will come to realize that when the student is ready to receive deeper spiritual insight and understanding ***'the teacher will appear.'***

With those words, MrJames remembers they were the final words spoken to him by Grandma; and the closing words from Teacher on the seventeenth day. She had said to me:

'Baby, unto whomsoever much understanding and insight is given' (Luke 12:48), and just exactly the same way as she had done the day before she returned to the eternal realms, Grandma stopped in the middle of her sentence.

However, at that very moment it was the vibrating voice of Teacher, in the head of MrJames, continuing with her sentence, saying; "YoungMan," just like Grandfather Richard would call after me: "MrJames, you are one of the whomsoever, and readers of Proverbs become a whomsoever as well.

Continuing on, Teacher said: "much will be required, expected, and demanded of you (Luke 12:48), and readers will be responsible for much as well. Primarily, each of you must need to identify what is the unique divinely created purpose that is reflected in your life blueprint."

A thought from MrJames LifeCoach on Proverbs 18:

Several verses in this chapter further establish the standard that there is an eternal (forever) connection between the lips, mouth, tongue, heart, our thoughts, desires, and the words we speak (vs 1-8). The evil and wicked attitudes and dispositions of behavior emphasized in this chapter are connected like birds flocking together; a herd of cattle; a pack of wolves; school of fish; a swarm of bees; a colony of ants; or an army of frogs. Negative manifesting emotions and behaviors such as: deceitfulness, lying, stealing, disrespect, slothfulness, selfishness, perversion of speech, violence, idleness, foolishness, shame, and potential consequences associated with the words (seeds and fruit) of the mouth.

This chapter of Proverb introduces more harvesting outcomes forecasted to follow and travel along with the wicked; and budding from the seeds (words) of the mouth. But, as our hearts, our mind, and our will yield to and align with the will of our divinely created life purpose; then our thoughts will produce positive and successful outcomes, increased understanding, and lead us to living in the reflection of the blueprint of our divinely created purpose.

The voice of chapter 18 communicates using no uncertain terms; is straightforward; and is distinctly clear that many life pitfalls and entanglements can be avoided by keeping a guard on our mouth; by seeking out and finding our chosen life companion (spouse); showing forth ourselves ***friendly*** and that we may value and be worthy of friends and friendships.

The ultimate intent of the art of living challenge of reading from Proverbs daily is to introduce readers to being accountable to themselves and a better way of living; fully focused on living life as a reflection of the blueprint of the preordained divinely thought-out-beforehand created purpose for their lives; and to strongly encourage readers to accept all of life's experiences as beneficial to that divine process.

The initial primitive insights of twelve-year-old MrJames, from over five decades ago; and after many real-life experiences in the art of living, has become '10 Absolute Core Beliefs' of his life.

In the construct (make-up) of his present reality, MrJames discovered skillful Godly wisdom to be absolute eternal truth on which to build a life immersed in the blueprint of a divinely created purpose for living life.

MrJames continues to encourage readers to read Proverbs for ***themselves*** that they may identify important insights; special repeated instructions; intimately hear, and consciously receive intended messages that are hidden within the words of the Proverbs (2 Tim 3:16-17). After voluntarily deciding to spend investments of personal time reading Proverbs; MrJames was gently led, gradually persuaded, enticed, and invited to apply skillful Godly wisdom from Proverbs to the art of living.

Then, after deciding to do so, he began to mirror, duplicate, and reflect the blueprint of a divinely created purpose for his life coming to view in the construct (make-up) of his reality; and producing positive outcomes in his art of living quest and journey.

Finally, prompted and divinely influenced from the eternal realms; Grandma, Grandfather Richard, and Teacher would consistently remind MrJames again and again, that on this chosen path: 'the Sovereign—All-knowing, All-powerful, Ever-present, Most High God—Our Heavenly Father,

Supreme Creator, and Master Designer of ALL that exists directs our path; and yielding to HIS will leads us to become what we were destined to become.'

Remember: He who knows and knows he knows is wise. However, he who knows but knows not that he knows is yet still unlearned, immature, and ignorant. Therefore, Stop—pause; Listen—tune-in; Observe—just do it; Think—review and reflect; Retain—remember that applying skillful Godly wisdom to the art of living life is the roadway leading to Prudence—caution, Providence—foresight, and Divine Destiny. There is no other way!

In the name of Jesus Christ. Amen.

***** CHANGE *****

PERMANENT CHANGE IS EFFECTIVE:

ONLY WHEN

THE NEED 4 CHANGE

Plus

THE INCENTIVE 2 CHANGE IS

EX—CEPT—IT

&

THEN

M—PLE—MENT— IT

21

DAY 19 - COUNSEL WITH OTHERS

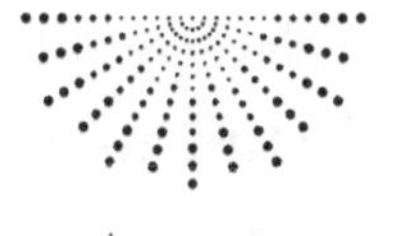

PROVERBS 19

Today is the nineteenth consecutive day of the month. Who answered the challenge the first day of reading the corresponding numbered chapter from Proverbs each of those days. This challenge to seek wisdom under the title of the art of living was issued by MrJames LifeCoach when he asked readers to make a voluntary investment in themselves by directing intentional conscious efforts in a pursuit to obtain skillful Godly wisdom by committing daily to read from The Book of Proverbs—also known as The Book of Wisdom.

Usually, that is for nearly six decades, MrJames has preferred reading from the King James Version of the Holy Bible. However, for the most recent five years, his daily insights on Proverbs are based also on New King James, New International Version, New Living Translation, and Amplified Classic Version of the Holy Bible. MrJames

LifeCoach describes "The Art of Living" as insistent, persistent determination, and an unrelenting continuation to push forward in your life quest to become what you were created to become; no matter what life may throw at you along the way.

In doing so, he believes real-life experiences have a mysterious aspect, and real-life experiences have an uncanny ability to serve as an effective tutor in the art of living our divinely created purpose; having learned from personal real-life experiences that when the student is ready to live in divine purpose, the teacher will appear.

MrJames insistently emphasizes that these experiences include pleasant and not so pleasant tests, trials, tribulations, and also life-shaking and life-shattering challenges, happenings, and incidents. Eventually, in the psychology of the aging process, we come to acknowledge on the life journey that we are getting too soon old, too late smart; our timetable, choices, and life chances are gradually drifting away like sands through the proverbial hourglass.

<u>A thought from MrJames LifeCoach on Proverbs 19:</u>

Several verses in several chapters in The Book of Wisdom—Proverbs—establish an eternal and everlasting connection between the lips, mouth, tongue, heart, our thoughts, our desires, and the words we speak. However, the emphasis in this chapter suggests that being "foolish, self-confident, dishonest, deceitful, irreverent, scornful—ridiculing and teasing (making fun of) and being slothful—lazy and idle are actions and conduct that is nothing less than perversions of Godly character. Furthermore, within this same chapter, a firm warning against liars and those who bear false witness is repeated at least twice.

This chapter of Proverb also establishes that a prudent wife —sensible and wise; integrity, healthy self-love, getting of Godly wisdom; decency and discretion, and true friendships are divine gifts from the Supreme Creator—God—Heavenly Father—Master Designer of all that exists. However, HE knows our thoughts, the motives behind and underneath our thoughts, and HE sees our insincere, foolish, rebellious, and knuckleheaded acts as well.

However, as our hearts, mind, choices, desires and as our will aligns with the will of our divinely created life purpose; our thoughts begin to produce positive and desired successful outcomes, increases our spiritual understanding, and leads us to live in the reflection of the blueprint of our divinely created purpose.

The voice of Proverbs in each of the thirty-one chapters in the book communicates in no uncertain terms, straightforward and distinctly clear that many life pitfalls can be avoided.

Readers are repeatedly called to alert, warned, and cautioned that keeping guard over our mouth; perverseness out of our heart, and seeking a chosen companion (spouse), showing ourselves to be "friendly" that we may be worthy of godly friendships; and skillfully seeking after and observing Godly wisdom can protect from and help to keep evil away.

A foundation of more than six decades of real-life experiences persuades LifeCoach to constantly remind clients that skillful godly wisdom—and words, thoughts, daily conduct, and how we apply godly wisdom is significant in the art of living, and "knowledge is power".

Therefore, He is ever reminding readers that the search for skillful godly wisdom— "she" must be desired, looked for, pursued, respected, and valued if we are to produce a reflective life of the blueprint of our divinely created purpose.

The original unpolished simple insights of twelve-year-old MrJames, from nearly six decades ago, and after many real-life pleasant and not so pleasant experiences in the art of living; has become his "10 Absolute Core Beliefs" and he has found them to be eternal truths upon which to build a life that will reflect an eternal blueprint of a divine purpose.

Finally, as always, MrJames the LifeCoach reminds readers again: God—Our Heavenly Father, Supreme Creator, and Master Designer of all that exists "directs our paths" and will lead us to become what we were destined to become. And, if readers do all that we can do, trust in HIM that all things will work together so we will accomplish and fulfill our divinely created purpose; becoming a reflection of the blueprint of their divinely created purpose.

Remember: Knowledge is power. He who knows and knows

he knows is wise. He who knows, lives, conducts, and does according to that which he know is wiser. However, he who knows but knows not that he knows is yet still unlearned, immature, and ignorant.

Therefore, Stop—pause; Listen—tune-in; Observe—just do it; Think—reflect; and Retain— remember; applying skillful Godly wisdom is the roadway leading to prudence, providence, and divine destiny. This is the only roadway to prudence, providence, and divine destiny. There is no other way!

In the name of Jesus Christ. Amen.

22

TWO SHALL BECOME ONE

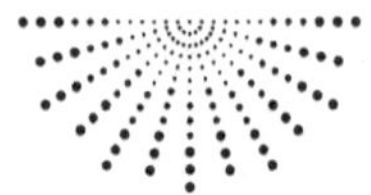

WISDOM FROM THE AGES

Two Shall Become One
Gen 2:24; Matt 19:5; Mark 10:8-9; Eph 5:31; 2 Cor 6:14

To understand a link from our physical world into the spiritual world, reflect upon marriage—matrimony, sacred, holy union of male and female. No one can take it upon oneself to "put asunder"—forcefully set apart what God puts together. Therefore, the actions and consequences of the actions of one flesh cannot be separated from acts or consequences of the other.

"The two shall become one flesh."

Thus, whatever affects one flesh infects the other. The marriage covenant binds two individuals together to become one flesh. Joined as one through marriage, they both will reap what is sown by the other. As one flesh, the actions sown by one produce consequences to be reaped by the other, regardless of the sower.

"The two shall become one flesh."

Therefore, "do not be unequally yoked to unbelievers;" unbelievers can produce a harvest that is in opposition to believers. Hence, only if one partner is doing the sowing, both can reap consequences. Thus, "as for me and my house, we will serve the [living God]."

"The two shall become one flesh."

Two Shall Become One
James 3:2, 17; Job 1:1; Matt 5:48; Isaiah 54:17; Alma 41:10

Ongoing sinful acts of one; unacknowledged, un- confessed, un-repented, un-amended, and un-forgiven breed undesired fruit in marriage. Sinful fruit, allowed to ripen, produces a harvest of tribulation—trials, tests, torment, and chaos in marriage.

Sinful acts and "wickedness" come by way of Lucifer—Satan —Devil—Father of Lies. Therefore, wickedness can never lead to nor will evil ever become happiness. Always remember: "The two shall become one flesh."

One spouse is sewing, they both reap; even if only the other is sewing and both will reap. Two, now joined as one; each sowing seeds into one life that is now joined together. Although they are both unique individuals and they are formed, born, and developed separate; by way of the Sacred Covenant of Marriage between a Man and a Woman: "two become one flesh."

Two Shall Become One Flesh
One Man + One Woman
Two Fleshes
R 2 B 1
U R 2 B 1
Become One Flesh

Two Shall Become One Flesh
1+1=2
½ (1+1) = (2) ½
(½ x 1) + (½ x 1) = (2 x ½)
(½) + (½) = 1
1 = 1
Two Flesh CAN Join As One

Two Become One
If U R 2 B 1
U Must Multiply
Your Better Half
Two Shall Become ONE

M.A.N. + WOM.A.N.
M-ature A-ltogether N-ewcreation
BORN AGAIN
+
G O D—THE Creator-Master Designer
=
A DIVINE SPECIES
Greater is HE that is within thee.

23
DAY 20 - ABUSE NOT THE POOR

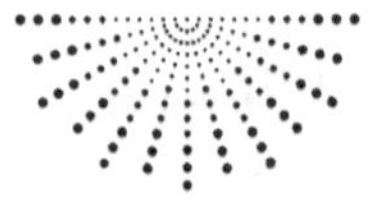

PROVERBS 20

Today is the twentieth consecutive day this month of reading the corresponding numbered chapter for the date of the month from The Book of Proverbs. The task to seek wisdom, titled "The Art of Living," was issued asking readers to make a time investment in themselves, challenging whomever to focus and direct their pursuit of obtaining skillful Godly wisdom and commit to reading a chapter daily from The Book of Proverbs—also known as The Book of Wisdom.

Since the age of twelve, nearly six decades have passed as MrJames has been consistently reading from the King James Bible Version. This process of daily reading the chapter from Proverbs matching the date of the month, MrJames has consistently repeated for nearly five years. However, for these insights, he has included reading from the New King James, New International, New Living Translation; and the

Amplified Classic Version of the Holy Bible; and he describes "The Art of Living" as insistent, persistent determination, an unrelenting continuation to push forward in your life quest; to become what you were created to become, no matter what life may throw at you along the way.

MrJames believes real-life experiences have a mysterious ability to serve as effective tutors in the art of living; as he has experienced that when a student is ready to live out their divine purpose, the teacher will appear. He urges readers to ponder, consider, reflect upon, embrace, and internalize a life-view that accepts the basic core belief of the existence of a Supreme Eternal Creator—God—Heavenly Father—Master Designer of all that exists; and he controls all life experiences.

MrJames believes all life experiences are strategically placed, timely, and divinely appointed in the span of the life course; and include pleasant and not so pleasant; tests, trials, tribulations, life-shaking challenges, and life-shattering experiences as well. However, all experiences are tailor-made with purpose, meaning, and come with valuable life lessons intermingled, interwoven, inherent, and connected to the experience.

<u>A thought from MrJames LifeCoach on chapter 20:</u>

There are several unique verses in this specific chapter of The Book of Wisdom; that are no more than a list of alarming outcries against narcissistic personality traits, such as: grandiose (high flaunting) pride, deceitful lying, vows of revenge, self-righteousness, laziness and oversleeping, dishonesty, unjust measurements in weights and scales, fraud, unrighteous judgments, mocking disrespectful conduct toward that which is holy. Although the words fool, foolish, naive, or immature are not used in this chapter; their voice rings out between the lines, and in the descriptions used throughout this chapter.

Notice within this same chapter, there is a billowing repeated warning against deceitful—hollow weights and scales, and that clearly denounced these acts as abomination in the eyes of the Most High God—Our Heavenly Father, Supreme Creator, Master Designer of all that exists. It is He who knows our thoughts, our motives, our intent underneath our thoughts, and He foresees our insincere, foolish, and even our knucklehead acts.

Remember, the intent of the challenge is to introduce readers to the concept, notion, and idea of holding themselves accountable to a better way in the art of living. A higher-way that is fully focused on living life as a reflection of the blueprint of the preordained divinely created purpose for their lives.

Dr. M.L. King, Jr. taught that: "There is, somewhere in the realms of eternity, a blueprint of each of our lives, and all life events and happenings are on that blueprint." As we discover and travel the higher-way in the art of living; we become a reflection of that eternal blueprint.

Accepting the existence of an eternal life blueprint as an absolute truth; MrJames believes the million-dollar question then becomes: Will readers voluntarily apply the wisdom discovered, gained, and gleaned from reading the Proverbs; to their art of living quest; and will they yield-to and follow the higher-way that leads them to become a "reflection of the blueprint" (Jer 1:5), of the divinely created purpose for their lives?

Finally, as always, MrJames reminds himself and all readers as well: The Most High God—Our Heavenly Father, Supreme Creator, Master Designer of all that exists "directs our paths" and from the eternal realms of existence He has navigated each of us to the crossing road of The Book of Proverbs. Now, to readers who have answered the challenge, your questions are:

1. Will you willingly put-off natural man tendencies?

(John 3:3; Mosiah 3:19);

2. Will you willingly accept HIS will—last will and testament —not your will? (Rom 12:1-2; D&C 8:26);

3. Will you willingly submit to the "consecrated afflictions" on the divine blueprint of your life? (Rom 8:37-37; 2 Ne 2:2);

4. Will you willingly allow the unfolding of the divine art of living plan and the blueprint for your life; designed by the Master Designer of ALL that exists; Sovereign Most High God; Our Heavenly Father; to be manifested as a construct

of physical reality on Earth, as it is in Heaven? (Jer 29:11; Matt 6:10; 1 Ne 3:7, 4:6)

And, if we do all that we can do, trust all things to work together (Rom 8:28; D&C 98:3), so we will accomplish and fulfill our divinely created purpose; and become a reflection of the divine blueprint of our existence.

It has been said by notable self-proclaimed philosopher Tom Sawyer: "The two most important days in a person's life are: the day of their birth; and the day they find out why they were born." Highly intrigued by the profound and thought-provoking question, MrJames realized, placing the answers side by side that most people have spent considerably more time thinking about birthday and celebration, than why they were born in the first place.

However, nearly all would likely agree the more important answer relates to the why you were born answer. Therefore, MrJames asks all readers this question only so that they may think, ponder and contemplate—meditate on their 2nd day answer. To thine own self be true: How much time have you actually spent pondering the divine purpose for which you were created? In other words: "Unto what purpose came you into this world; and in its essence, what is the divinely created purpose of your life and existence?"

Remember: Knowledge is power. He who knows and knows he knows is wise. He who knows, who lives, who conducts, and who does according to that which he knows is wiser.

However, he who knows but knows not that he knows is yet still unlearned, immature, and ignorant.

Therefore, Stop—pause; Listen—tune-in; Observe—just do it; Think—reflect; and Retain—remember; applying skillful Godly wisdom is the road leading to prudence, providence and divine destiny. This is the only roadway to prudence, providence and divine destiny. There is no other way!

In the name of Jesus Christ. Amen.

Life Is:
Lived Forward
1 Moment, 1 Hour, 1 Week, 1 Month
1 Year - 1 Decade – 1 Century- 1 Millennium
One-DAY-At-A-Time

But, Life Is: Understood Backwards;
As we Reflect, Recall, Review, Re-visit;

And; Ponder all our past
Life-Shaking & Life-Shattering
& Real-Life Events

Then We Discover
Tailor-Made Experiences
For Our Eternal Good

24

DAY 21 - SITS HIGH, LOOKS LOW

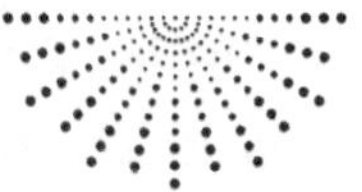

PROVERBS 21

Today is the twenty-first day this month, reading the corresponding numbered chapter from Proverbs that coincides with the date of the month. This challenge to seek wisdom, titled "The Art of Living," was issued by MrJames LifeCoach. He asked readers to make a time investment in themselves, directing their pursuit of obtaining skillful godly wisdom, by committing to read one chapter daily from The Book of Proverbs—The Book of Wisdom. He has now repeated this daily task himself for over five years.

Exactly what does it mean: "The Art of Living"? LifeCoach describes "The Art of Living" as insistent, persistent determination, and unrelenting continuation to push forward in your life quest to become what you were created to become, no matter what life may throw at you along the way. MrJames adamantly believes the art of living in real-life requires that each person ponders, considers, reflects upon, embraces, and internalizes a life-view that accepts a basic core belief of the existence of a Sovereign Most High God—Our Heavenly Father, Supreme Eternal Creator, Master Designer of all that exists who is in control of all life experiences.

Therefore, in the construction of life realities, our experiences will include both; pleasant and the not so pleasant; tests, trials, tribulations, and even life-shaking, and life- shattering challenges and experiences as well. As such, all life experiences are tailor-made with divine purpose and meaning, and there are valuable life lessons interwoven into the experiences.

Eventually, in the psychology of the aging process, we likely will come to that place where we acknowledge, during the life journey, that we are getting "too soon old but too late smart" and our present life timetable becomes shortened, our quality of life chances are gradually drifting away; and like sands through the hourglass, our time on this Earth is winding down.

<u>A thought from MrJames LifeCoach on Proverbs 21:</u>

Several unique verses in chapter twenty-one of Proverbs partly highlight, 10 Absolute Core Beliefs of MrJames, appropriately more in this one chapter than all the others. One such belief, mentioned in the first three verses, is also repeated in the closing verses of Chapter 21; and it reiterates, reinforces, and highlights one of his core beliefs.

Specifically, these verses confirm that the Supreme Creator —God— Heavenly Father—Master Designer of all that exist is Sovereign—HE has final say In matters of life and death; and HE is in absolute control of all things (Abra 4:18).

The writer in this chapter strengthens, deepens belief in, significantly establishes, and teaches with examples that this Sovereign control includes all outcomes, in all circumstances and situations; including the pleasant and not so pleasant; hard tests and trials of life; and especially the unavoidable life-shaking, and sometimes life-shattering ones. LifeCoach points out that twice the writer in this chapter recognizes the chaos, turmoil, discontent, frustration, and pure agony of life with a "contentious," fault-finding, argumentative, narcissistic spouse in the house—woman or man.

Furthermore, throughout the entire chapter, the writer affirms diligence, righteousness, sincere actions, and sound behaviors of integrity in such a way as to illuminate negative outcomes, and opposing views against pleasure-seeking, lying, laziness, ill -gotten gain, and portrays human wisdom in opposition to that which is holy. Righteousness is the rewardable, preferred, acceptable way of the Supreme Creator—God—Heavenly Father—Master Designer of all that exist; and HE it is who knows our thoughts, our motives; and foresees our insincere, foolish, and knuckleheaded rebellious acts.

"Circumstances, situations,
and events of life,
no matter how difficult;

Nor the people
around Me
in life, and no matter
their attitudes and
dispositions;

They do not
make me the
way I am.

[*BUT*],

REAL-LIFE
Experiences; real-happenings;
and my reactions,

just reveal the way I am.

[Dr. Sam Peeples].

25
PEACE SERENITY CONTENTMENT

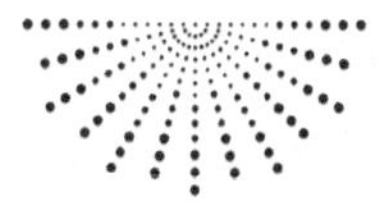

WEEK THREE

Finally, just as always MrJames begins to remind readers; but no sooner than he began to do so, and to his surprise, Teacher appeared present in his conscious awareness and HE was using his inaudible voice. He said, "MrJames, I perceive in you a tendency to discard the descriptive titles of Deity that you have repeated for three weeks to readers who answered the art of living challenge on the first day.

The importance and significance for readers of Proverbs to be reminded of each individual and distinct title of Deity and Divinity can never be emphasized enough in the art of living. This primary foundational belief in the existence of a Sovereign, Supreme, Most High Deity must need be understood, accepted, and believed by readers in order to displace erroneous beliefs about infinite intelligence and All-powerful God." ...(for a moment there was eerie silence)...

Internally, feeling somewhat perplexed about the silence and thinking to himself; MrJames realized for the first time that Teacher could perceive his thoughts.

Just as MrJames was becoming aware of his new insight, Teacher entered his mind and said, "MrJames, yes, I can perceive your thoughts because constant reading and study of Proverbs build connection to the eternal realms within the reader. But you, MrJames, are ready, just like Angel DEEmyrun and Grandma announced to all Guardian Angels when Grandma escorted DEEmyrun back to his eternal home."

Teacher continued: "MrJames, the silence is because you are still listening with your ears instead of perceiving with your heart—inner-essence of your being (Prov 22:17-19). In the silence, you must need to feel the message from behind your eyes and between your ears, just like Grandma told you it would happen." MrJames felt as if he was hearing the words from long ago when Grandma said, "Baby, you keep reading Proverbs and you will see without eyes, hear without ears (Prov 20:12), and you will know the truth of things deep inside of you" (Prov 22:20-21).

It was in that very moment; when MrJames knew what Grandma had been saying to him that day; and Teacher interrupted his thinking and said, "MrJames, constant reading Proverbs, applying the learned insights in the art of living, and encouraging others to do the same, has raised your conscious awareness in preparation for the most important phase of your divine life journey (Psalm 73:24).

I am Teacher, each time after the silence (Prov 17:27-28) you are becoming a higher vibrating, and a more self-actualize being, elevated in the consciousness of your present existence.

If you continue to read and study The Book of Proverbs with delight (Psalm 37:4); I am Teacher, I will return to you at an appointed time."

MrJames thought Teacher departed, but then felt him saying: "MrJames, remember you must need not get weary (Gal 6:9) when repeating the titles of Deity; keep reminding readers, just like Guardian Angels reminded you. I am Teacher, and I know you want to know why; I will explain when THE Source of Infinite Intelligence gives me the word."

It was gradual, but this time MrJames no longer perceived the presence of Teacher; and therefore he knew that Teacher was gone. However, this time there was not the total and complete silence that usually flowed in the wake of the quietness that came after HIS departure. But instead, there came into the conscious awareness of MrJames, an overwhelming sensation of peace contentment, calmness, and a genuine feeling of relaxing satisfaction.

Then, suddenly rising-up out of seemingly nowhere; and just like a pleasant, soft, cool, and refreshing breeze on a sunny day; incoming on the mind-screen of MrJames, and being read in a detectable but inaudible voice of Mother Iola; he saw, heard, and felt the words of his mother's favorite poem.

Recognizing the familiar words, MrJames remembered his Grandma Inez had said, "Baby, your Mother Iola accepted, believed, and had internalized the poem as an unadulterated —pure and virtuous direct message straight from the eternal realms. Mother Iola had applied the principles of the poems in the art of living.

However, the original words of the poem had been found in Rome, Italy in 1692 (revised 1927); on the walls of Old Saint Paul's Church; and the message in the poem had been left there by an "anonymous author."

Since the death of Grandma in 1971; and following the tragic death of Mother Iola in 1979, MrJames always felt his Guardian Angel Mothers and Grandmothers were instrumental in delivering to him, these words:

Desiderata – Max Ehrmann

Go placidly amid the noise and haste, and remember what peace there may be in silence. As far as possible, without surrender, be on good terms with all persons. Speak your truth quietly and clearly; and listen to others, even the dull and ignorant; they too have their story. Avoid loud and aggressive persons, they are vexations to the spirit.

If you compare yourself with others, you may become vain and bitter; for always there will be greater and lesser persons than yourself. Enjoy your achievements as well as your plans. Keep interested in your own career, however humble; it is a real possession in the changing fortunes of time. Exercise caution in your business affairs; for the world is full of trickery. But let this not blind you to what virtue there is; many persons strive for high ideals; and everywhere life is full of heroism.

Be yourself. Especially, do not feign affection. Neither be cynical about love; for in the face of all aridity and disenchantment, it is perennial as the grass. Take kindly the counsel of the years, gracefully surrendering the things of youth. Nurture strength of spirit to shield you in sudden misfortune. But do not distress yourself with imaginings. Many fears are born of fatigue and loneliness. Beyond a wholesome discipline, be gentle with yourself. You are a child of the universe, no less than the trees and the stars; you have a right to be here! And, whether or not it is clear to you, no doubt the universe is unfolding as it should. Therefore, be at peace with God, whatever you conceive Him to be, and whatever your labors and aspirations, in the noisy confusion of life keep peace with your soul. Even with all its sham, drudgery, fraud, scams, identity theft, and broken dreams, it is still a beautiful world. Consider it all joy. Be cheerful. Strive to be happy.

In the name of Jesus Christ. Amen.

26
DAY 22 - WEALTH W/O TOIL

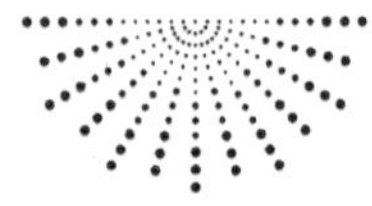

PROVERBS 22

Today, readers and listeners who answered the initial challenge on day one begin the twenty-second consecutive day and enter the third week of reading the corresponding numbered chapter for the date of the month from The Book of Proverbs. This challenge and invitation were to seek wisdom, titled "The Art of Living," and was issued by MrJames as the first day of the month began.

MrJames challenged readers to invest time in themselves, asking readers to direct their pursuit of knowledge to obtaining skillful Godly wisdom and commit to read one chapter daily from The Book of Proverbs—a.k.a. The Book of Wisdom. MrJames has repeated this daily discipline consistently for nearly five years.

Exactly what is the meaning of "The Art of Living"? MrJames describes "The Art of Living" as insistent, persistent determination, and unrelenting continuation to push forward in life. MrJames LifeCoach has learned from real-life experiences that "when the student is ready" to live out their divine purpose, then and only then the teacher will appear."

MrJames urges each reader of Proverbs to ponder, consider, reflect upon, embrace, and internalize a life-view that accepts, as a basic core belief in the actual existence of The Most High God—Supreme Eternal Creator—Heavenly Father—Master Designer of all that exists; and that HE is absolutely in control of all life experiences.

Eventually, in the psychology of aging process, we come to that place where we acknowledge that we are getting "too soon old, too late smart" and our timetable of life and our life chances, like sand in the hour glass of our life journey, is gradually fading away.

A thought from MrJames LifeCoach on Proverbs 22:

The message of several verses within this twenty-second chapter of Proverbs affirms and confirms the truth of words from three church hymns. Each title serves not only as an excellent summary of the chapter, but appropriately the words of each of the three titles presents a proverbial ***"Reader's Digest"*** condensed synopsis, summary, and conclusion for the entire Book of Proverbs.

The first:

How Gentle God's Commands—How gentle God's commands! How kind his precepts are! Come, cast your burdens on the Lord and trust his constant care. Beneath his watchful eye, his saints securely dwell. That hand which bears all nature up shall guard his children well. Why should this anxious load press down your weary mind? Haste to your heavenly father's throne and sweet refreshment find.

The Second:

Choose the Right—Choose the right when a choice is placed before you. In the right, the Holy Spirit guides; and its light is forever shining over you, when in the right your heart confides. Choose the right, let no spirit of digression overcome you in the evil hour. There is the right, and the wrong to every question; be safety through inspiration's power. Choose the right, there is peace in righteous doing. Choose the right, there's safety for the soul. Choose the right, in all labors you are pursuing, let God and heaven be your goal. Let wisdom mark the way before. Choose the right, And God will bless you ever more.

The Third:

Do What is Right—Do what is right the day dawn is breaking, hailing a future of freedom and light. Angels above us are silent notes taking …then do what is right, and let the consequence follow. Do what is right the shackles are falling; lightened by hope soon there will cease the galling. Truth goes onward, then do what is right…be faithful and fearless...Eyes that are wet now ere long will be tearless. Blessings await you in doing what's right! Battle for our freedom in spirit and might; and look ye forth till tomorrow; God will protect you, so do what is right and let the consequence follow.

Need MrJames say any more to the readers who continue to answer your commitment to the challenge? The Supreme Creator—God—Heavenly Father—Master Designer of all that exists has the final say, the absolute authority, and HE is in total control of all things. This chapter affirms the pathway of diligence, righteousness, sincere actions, and behaviors of integrity as preferred ways of God—Supreme Creator— Heavenly Father—Master Designer of all that exists. And it is this specific chapter that establishes that it is HE who knows our thoughts, our motives, and foresees our insincere, foolish, stubborn, and even our knucklehead rebellious acts.

MrJames intentionally, consciously, and constantly reminds readers that knowledge is power: and words, thoughts, our daily conduct; and how we apply Godly wisdom is significant in the art of living outcomes. Therefore, skillful godly wisdom—"she" must need be desired, looked for, pursued, respected, observed, valued, and internalized if we are to produce the desired life that will be reflective of the blueprint of our divinely created purpose.

Remember, the intent of the challenge from MrJames is to introduce and hold readers to be accountable to themselves to choose the better way to live; Life and death are in the power of the tongue—choose life (Prov 18:21). Continue your reading of The Book of Proverbs; your study of sacred Holy Scriptures; and then decide to become fully focused on living your life as a reflection of the blueprint of the preordained divinely created purpose for your life; and accept all life experiences as beneficial to that divine process.

Finally, as always, MrJames reminds himself and readers again: God—Our Heavenly Father, Our Creator, Supreme Being, and Master Designer of all that exists "directs our paths" and will lead us to become what we were destined to become.

And if we do all that we can do, trust all things to work together so we will accomplish and fulfill our divinely created purpose; and become a reflection of the blueprint of our divinely created purpose.

Life Decisions

Early in the journey through life, a person finds themselves at a crossroad, AND must choose one of two roads of great highways.

- THE right, leading to progress and happiness
- THE wrong, leading to retardation and sorrow.

There exists an eternal law that each human soul, through the choices they make, will shape their own destiny.

Our Success or Failure, Peace, Happiness or Misery; Depends on the choices we make each day.

Remember: He/She who knows and knows he/she knows is wise. He who knows, speaks, acts, conducts, and lives life according to the truths he/she knows is wiser. However, he/she who knows but knows not that he/she knows is yet still unlearned, immature, and ignorant. Therefore, Stop—Pause; Listen—Heed; Observe—Do; Think—Reflect; Retain—Remember F.R.O.G. and Fully Rely On God.

As this chapter ends, MrJames is filled with the presence of an overwhelming influence from the eternal realms. "MrJames" is what he hears throughout his inner being: "I, Teacher, am sent to give you deeper knowledge, understanding, and insight on Deity—Sovereign Most High God. There are idol gods, Greek gods, mystical gods, and gods of darkness; this is all truth.

However, Godly wisdom teaches of The Sovereign—ALL Powerful, All Knowing, Ever-Present God—The Ruling Authority over and above all things (Ex 20:3; Rom 13:1; 14:11, Heb. 6:13; Mosiah 27:31); The Most High God—no other God; nothing too hard for God (Jer. 32:17); believe that HE exists and rewards diligence" (Heb. 11:6).

Teacher continues: "Come closer MrJames so you can get understanding (Prov. 4:7); because understanding Deity is the building block to construct any foundation for spiritual enlightenment, understanding, and insights. Readers and believers must need to know the true identity, roles, and characteristics of God—THE Most High God; THE Supreme Being; Infinite Intelligence, Master Designer of ALL that exists, and that HE, and HIM only has ABSOLUTE control of ALL things. The enemy of Mankind distorts the true identity of God and that can hinder the progression and the building of intimacy in our relationship with Deity."

Furthermore, Teacher explained, "erroneous belief related to Deity confuses the true nature of HIS role in the art of living; creates cognitive dissonance—perplexing complexity, and uncertainty in the world about HIS role in our lives."

MrJames never uttered a sound, however he was consciously aware that he had assured Teacher that he understood. But Teacher said: "Come closer MrJames; I know what you do and do not know; I even know what you think and why you think the thoughts that you think."

Thus, Teacher said to MrJames: "Pray first, aim high, and stay focused on sharing divine insights you have received from your six decades of experiences; and continue encouraging readers and listeners to remain diligent as they continue to rise up in answer to the art of living challenge; and a marvelous work will be done in their lives. Now MrJames, just for now, Teacher will say no more."

MrJames begins to be consciously aware that he is becoming filled with the presence of an overwhelming influence he recognizes as a connection to the eternal realms; and he feels as if words are swelling up from the inside of himself. MrJames is under the impression that he is thinking silently to himself; at least until he heard the words come forth out of his mouth. Although; in his current reality no one was physically present with him; he started to speak as if he was addressing an audience of unseen readers and listeners; as if they were present and within the sound of his voice.

Lean-in my dear friends, gather all around, incline your eyes, ears, and attention forward that you may hear my words. I must need to tell you that after more than six decades of life experiences; more than five years of daily reading Proverbs; and uncounted hours spanning across nearly six decades of art of living life experiences.

During that time, I have been studying words of God from Sacred Holy Scriptures; listening, following, talking to myself, likening scriptures unto myself, and relating the words of ancient and modern- day prophets, seers, and revelators to the art of living.

Keeping those words in your mind; I, MrJames, testify to readers, hearers, and listeners of my words that it is by voluntarily deciding to invest time in oneself, firmly committing to seeking after and obtaining skillful Godly wisdom; is evidence-based and proven to be a higher roadway that leads men to prudence—carefulness, providence—foresight, and divine—preordained destiny in the art of living. This is not only the only way; but there is not a right way to do a wrong thing. To these things I testify;

and from the eternal realms I know to be true. God is no respecter of persons (Act 10:28,34-35); therefore you may know of this truth as well.

In the name of Jesus Christ. Amen.

27

DAY 23 - WICKEDNESS, NEVER HAPPINESS

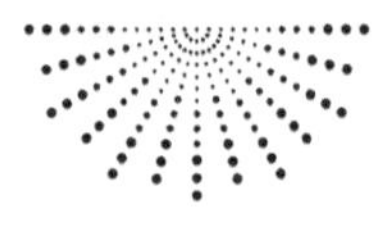

PROVERBS 23

Today is the twenty-third consecutive day this month of daily reading the corresponding numbered chapter of Proverbs for the same date of the month. MrJames boldly challenged and passionately asked readers to make a time investment in themselves, asking readers to direct their pursuit of obtaining skillful godly wisdom by committing to read one chapter daily from The Book of Proverbs—The Book of Wisdom.

He shares his insights from repeated daily reading the Proverbs for more than five years. His insights are based on nearly six decades of reading from the King James Version; as well as reading from New King James; New International; New Living Translation; and the Amplified Classic Version of the Holy Bible. Accept his challenge and review his insights, thoughts, and impressions related to the art of living (www.patreon.com/hardknocks).

MrJames describes "The Art of Living" as insistent, persistent determination, and unrelenting continuation to push forward in your life quest; to become what you were created to become, no matter what life may throw at you along the way. MrJames believes that when the student is ready to live out their divine purpose; it is then, and only then that the "teacher" will appear.

MrJames believes The Book of Proverbs confirms that life experiences are strategically placed, timely, and divinely appointed in the life course; and that life experiences are governed by the universal laws of cause and effect—a.k.a. "sowing and reaping."

Thus, it follows that all experiences are tailor-made with divine purpose, meaning, and valuable life lessons that are interwoven into the experiences; and will include pleasant, not so pleasant, tests and trials; tribulations, life-shaking and life-shattering challenges; and unforeseen experiences as well.

A thought from MrJames LifeCoach on Proverbs 23:

Readers who answered the challenge the first day are nearing the end of reading The Book of Proverbs, but this is one of the longer chapters. The writer repeats some of the related acts, conducts, dos, and do-not-do behaviors that are associated with negative consequences; reminding us to avoid immoral women (or men), listen to counsel from your parents, properly discipline children with the rod but do not abuse them; strive for knowledge, and seek to acquire skillful, Godly wisdom and understanding.

In a slightly humorous manner, the writer reminds and warns readers to avoid the pitfalls of work-a-holism, deceitful ambitious desires, perverted acts and behaviors, addictions, excessive alcohol consumption, and drunkenness. Equally important, from the Life Coach perspective, is that the initial focus of chapter twenty-three is about maintaining self-control, self-awareness, increasing mindfulness and present consciousness of real-time present surrounding circumstances.

With a blaring voice, readers are warned throughout the chapter: do not despise or reject Godly wisdom and knowledge; and Godly understanding cannot be verbally transferred to the foolish and ignorant—narcissistic; nor can Godly wisdom be gained and absorbed by osmosis—like a sponge, nor can it be soaked-up and absorbed into daily acts and behaviors of the unbelieving, the worldly, and the rebellious.

Receiving spiritual insight, and skillful Godly wisdom is like the opening of a treasure chest, in the art of living; filled with life-sustaining commodities; and it is only bestowed as a gift from God—Our Heavenly Father, Supreme Creator, and Master Designer of all that exists (D&C 130:20-21); showering down on qualifying recipients like dew from the heaven.

In conversation, MrJames confirms a belief in: spare the rod and spoil the child (vs 13-14), but he Does not condone and is not necessarily in agreement with some of the inhumane, and practical applications of the principle (literal beatings).

Yes, MrJames agrees with and accepts verse 13-14 of this chapter of proverbs; but not as one of his 10 Absolute Core Beliefs but acknowledges the need for proper discipline by the rod. But used symbolically like sideboards, boarders, perimeter markers, white lines down the highway of human development; and as a shepherd would you his rod—staff as a guide to steer away from danger, but not as an instrument to instill harm.

Therefore, MrJames urges caution in administering the rod because there is a possibility for improper disciplining by the rod, that can provoke one to anger; and produce unwanted, undesired, and unintended negative consequences as well. As such, MrJames believes the effectiveness of discipline by the rod is contingent upon method, severity, attitude, intention, and motivation behind the act of disciplining.

A foundation of more than six decades of real-life experiences persuades MrJames the to constantly remind clients and readers; not just that knowledge is power, but the lack of knowledge—ignorance; according to Grandma and the Bible (Hosea 4:6); is what leads to destruction, defeat, and bondage; and how we apply this godly wisdom is significant in the art of living.

The originals, now considered elementary (Col 2:8) and primitive insights of twelve year old MrJames, came from nearly six decades ago. and after many real-life experiences in the art of living, today those insights have become "10 Absolute Core Beliefs" of his life.

Finally, as instructed from beyond the eternal realms; although he might just be talking to himself; MrJames reminds all of us again: Sovereign Most High God—Our Heavenly Father, Supreme Creator, and Master Designer of ALL that exists "directs our paths" and will lead us to become what we were destined to become. In the art of living, after doing all we can; readers must need to trust all things to work together for good, and readers will accomplish and fulfill their divinely created purpose; according to the eternal blueprint for their life.

Just as MrJames was about to close his review of this chapter, he recognized the incoming presence of Teacher saying: "Come closer MrJames, it is critical and must need be that you tell readers that the ***Enemy of Mankind—Spirit of Anti-Christ, Prince of the Air, Philosophy—Spirit of Human Understanding*** distorts the identity of God. The Enemy of Good—Father of Lies; also knows that uncertainty in the heart or just in the conscious and unconscious mind of believers, as it relates to who God is and our connection and relationship to HIM, will somewhat hinder the effectiveness of human communication with God."

With increasing decibels of sound vibration, Teacher continued: "Readers must need to know that uncertainty in belief is akin to unbelief. Similarly, a mother-to-be is either pregnant and expecting, or not pregnant and not expectant; but there is no such thing as being almost or somewhat pregnant.

Such is the case with uncertainty in faith and belief; faith and faithless, and belief and non-belief are both two sides of the same coin. Just like flipping coins in the air (Prov 16:33); eventually we must choose faith and belief, or remain faithless and unbelieving—neither hot nor cold (Rev 3:16)."

Suddenly, what appeared to be a glow or an aurora was in the room and it felt and even smelt like Grandfather Richard was actually there. TEACHER must be Grandfather, MrJames thought to himself; and incoming was increasing decibels of sound in the distinct recognizable and inaudible voice of Grandfather Richard.

Teacher said: "MrJames, accepting, remaining, and being classified lukewarm, almost pregnant, or almost persuaded to believe (Acts 26:28) produces a poignant oxymoron—is contradictory—dichotic—diametrically opposed, and is an unrealistic construct of reality, like residing between two realms of existence; like the make-believe substance of a fairy-tale of a spacious building in the sky."

The thoughts in my mind, momentarily interrupted the message from Teacher; and then I began to notice that there was an increase in the brightness of the outline of the aurora in the room. Seemingly, the brightness of the light, and the increasing decibels of sound from the eternal realms was related to the importance of the message about to be delivered, and MrJames turned his focus back to Teacher and the message.

Apparently aware of my change in focus, Teacher continued, in his decibel increased inaudible voice. Cognizant and aware, MrJames sensed a trembling vibration penetrating the area immediately surrounding his personal space.

Teacher resumed delivering his message, not hurriedly but with an obvious increased sense of urgency. However, quite calmly He began to speak: "MrJames, tell your readers that ***NOW*** faith is...... (Heb 11:1); not yesterday, not tomorrow for the frogs to be gone like Pharaoh insisted (Exodus 8:9-10), not last year, not in 1820 and 1830; not more than 2,024 years ago; but faith, belief and certainty is ***NOW;*** therefore real, authentic, stronghold breaking, mountain-moving faith is ***NOW!*** Always in the present moment mindfulness."

Said Teacher to me: "In the grand schemes of the art of living MrJames LifeCoach; the time is not now, but ***rat NOW!*** And you know by way of, and traveling through the art of living for more than six decades; unbelief frustrates developing the present-day mindfulness of total acceptance of our conscious contact with God, and the development of feelings of radiant intimacy towards God, in the art of living."

Fully attuned and absorbing the serious content and context of this message; MrJames literally began to lean forward as Teacher continued: "MrJames, the insights, truths and spiritual understandings that were bestowed upon you because you voluntarily chose to obey Grandma as you continued to read Proverbs and applied their teachings in the art of living."

MrJames thought to himself: I always obeyed Grandma, except one time when she told me about the "5 Frogs" in the pond that were sitting on a log. She said three frogs had decided to jump; but she insistently wanted me to go down to that pond three or four times to see how many frogs would be left sitting on the log? Even then, reluctantly MrJames had obeyed Grandma; but the smile on Grandma's face, and the lessons MrJames learned from the "5 Frogs" (see Death To Frogs by MrJames LifeCoach); is what he has long remembered and will likely never forget.

No sooner than when MrJames turned the attention of his mind back to receiving the message, Teacher continued again: "MrJames, you are expected and required (Matt 12:48) to identify, insert, and substitute out the erroneous beliefs, and displace the deceptive beliefs and philosophies of Man—worldly intellect; with absolute truths you have gained in the art of living; from Sacred Scriptures; from modern-day Prophets, Apostles, Teachers, and Inspired Leaders, and from your reading and study of the proverbs contained in The Book of Wisdom. These absolute truths and beliefs are to be substituted in place of the erroneous beliefs that are in the heart—core essence of some readers."

Talking to himself, MrJames thought; "Look-er-here Self, why me." Immediately the voice of Teacher said: "Why not you? MrJames, all life experiences; the pleasant—not so pleasant; the desired—no so desired; even the life-shaking and life-shattering ones has prepared you for a divine purpose. You, MrJames, the Student is ready; I, Teacher, was sent to appear to you. It is getting late on your timetable of the art of living; and much confusion remains in the hearts of many readers; but only because "they know not where to find truth" (D&C 123:11-12). MrJames became enveloped with a penetrating sensation of awareness, enlightenment, and insight that served to bring a sense of seriousness to the words that Teacher was communicating to him. Teacher continued: "MrJames, in The Book of Proverbs there are absolute truths about the art of living, the true nature of God; about our relationship to him; and about HIS role in our lives and in the art of living. Those same absolute truths can be revealed to the committed, devoted, consistent readers of Proverbs; as directed by, and in the foreordained, appointed, and in the due timing of the divine eternal blueprint of GOD—Sovereign, Most High God—Our Heavenly Father—The Father of Our Spirit—Breath of Life (Gen 2:7)."

MrJames, began sensing a familiar spirit of enlightenment, he realized that the most chosen title of reference used by Jesus, in the four recorded Gospel accounts of the life of Jesus, is: "Father, Heavenly Father, or Father in Heaven" (Matt 5:48; 6:9).

Continuing in talking to himself, MrJames thought: "I have always known that the relationship between God and Man was an intimate one; but now I see, readers must need to know that our relationship is a one-on-one connection to Deity—God. And, our inter-connectedness is best understood when seen in the light of the relationship that most responsible, caring, and devoted earthy fathers have with their children—Daddy-daughter; Father-son; and the most personal and intimate descriptive phrase of all is "Abba" [my Daddy], (Mark 14:26).

In essence we have an inherent birthright to call out to—not your Daddy, not to a collective Our Daddy—; but "Abba" is a phrase that literally means: my daughter Darnaisha has a God-given right to cry out to God saying I want ***"my Daddy"*** which is a much more personal and intimate outcry from a child, for their "own" father—Heavenly Father.

MrJames, continuing to talk to himself, said: I did not know everybody did not know God—Father of Humanity—Father of us all; but also Father—Master Designer of ALL that exists, and Father of the unique individual nature of each of HIS created Beings.

Just as MrJames reached the end of that thought; the presence of Teacher revealed an unsolicited answer: "Yes, that is true MrJames; but you received your insight, understanding, and knowledge of God from reading The Book of Proverbs. You must need tell readers that reading Proverbs helps to settle uncertainty surrounding truths related to the identity, nature, and role of God in the art of living. Tell them skillful Godly wisdom from Proverbs protects readers against the creation of dissonance—complexity, uncertainty in the art of living, and in the world about God—The Father, and about HIS role in our lives."

In his mind, MrJames affirmed his understanding of the message delivered to him by Teacher, and then he sensed Teacher had departed the present Earthly realm of existence; leaving MrJames to solemnly ponder the message.

Remember: He who knows and knows he knows is wise. However, he who knows but knows not that he knows is yet still unlearned, immature, and ignorant; to him who knows to do right and do it not, to him it is called sin (James 4:17); and it is foolish because you become your own worst enemy, and the resulting outcomes are only negative and self-defeating.

Therefore, Stop—Pause; Listen—Heed; Observe—Do; Think —Reflect; Retain—Remember; this is the roadway to prudence, providence and divine destiny. There is not a right way to do a wrong thing. Doing evil, willful wickedness will never be, nor produce happiness; it the contrary and in opposition to our divine nature and existence (Alma 41:4).

In the name of Jesus Christ. Amen.

Life Lessons

Trials, Tests, Obstacles, Failure, Rejection, Challenges, Griefs, Frustrations, and Disappointments.

The final outcome is never as worse as it seems it will be in the beginning. There is an unseen hand ALWAYS at work. Divine intervention is never late, Always on time, BUT rarely early. All you can do is all you can do; Then, and only then, is it all you can do.

"GREATNESS CAN ONLY BE ACHIEVED WHEN ALL THAT CAN BE DONE, HAS BEEN DONE."

28
DAY 24 - DIVINE PROTECTION

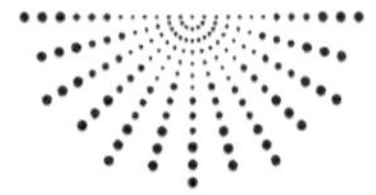

PROVERBS 24

Today is the twenty-fourth day this month, reading the corresponding numbered chapter from Proverbs. Only a few more days remaining in this month. MrJames may be talking to himself, but to all the readers who are stepping up, meeting this challenge, and are current for this chapter reading, I pray: "The Word shall not return void, but the Word from your study shall accomplish the thing in your life and prosper in the thing for which the Word was sent" (Isa 55:10-11).

This challenge to seek after wisdom, titled "The Art of Living," was issued by MrJames, LifeCoach. He invited readers to freely and voluntarily make a time investment in themselves, asking readers to focus and redirect the pursuit of gaining skillful Godly wisdom by committing to read one chapter daily from Proverbs—a.k.a. The Book of Wisdom.

MrJames has repeated this daily discipline for nearly five years. Accept the challenge, then review his thoughts and impressions (www.patreon.com/hardknocks).

A thought from MrJames LifeCoach on Proverbs 24:

Nearing the end of this chapter of Proverbs, the writer of this chapter continues listing the 30 additional verses containing skillful godly wisdom that he began listing in the previous chapter. When carefully reading through this chapter and the previous one, you will find skillful godly wisdom focused on genuine love, respect, and proper applications of acquired Godly wisdom. The wisdom and the experiences gained through the application of skillful godly wisdom can lead the enlightened individual to avoid and not be envious of evil men, their ways, nor their possessions.

These additional words of wisdom explain, among other things, that the sure way to construct a house—live your life —build your family, and to raise your children is upon a structure and foundation of moral and spiritual values. These components will not falter under the pressures of life and will endure the tests of time.

Skillful godly wisdom is a source of personal strength, and knowledge increases strength, and there is success and safety in “a multitude of counselors” (vs 6). Avoid the schemer or scorner—devious person who plots to do evil (vs 8-9). Within this inclusive collected group of 30 proverbs is the assertion and sense that we should welcome 'the day of adversity' as a way to reveal our personal spiritual strength or weakness (vs 10-12). The counsel from this chapter of Proverbs suggests we are to continue to move forward in the art of living; both in weak times and times of strength. Diligence in time of weakness as an exercise to develop us to become stronger in areas of weakness (2 Cor 12:9), but not meant to destroy or defeat us.

MrJames realizes that to some this counsel may seem somewhat contradictory; however, from his real-life experiences, he is confident and sure that we all have human weakness as an undeniable part of our makeup and wiring (Ether 12:27-28). Weakness is inherent to and within the construct that makes us human, assuring each human that neither of us is a saint. For it is written, even the righteous may fall seven times (vs 16), but this Proverb implies he will get up.

Therefore, when we seem prone to fall, and even though we may fail frequently; when life's temptations come upon us, we should be at ease; and knowing that as believers, even in our failures and weakness, we have been promised "His grace is sufficient" (2 Cor 12:9-10) and HE will stand in the gap of our weakness. Therefore, MrJames believes, as Proverbs implies; to fail, stumble, and fall under the natural pressures of the art of living is not what ultimately determines destiny. It is the action of diligent, determined, persist, rising-up, and refusing to stay down that determines final outcomes in the art of living.

In the art of living, this chapter in Proverbs suggests that readers must need to remember to keep getting up, brush yourself off, and keep moving forward. Godly wisdom from Proverbs reminds MrJames, since he might be talking to himself; that we should always place respect and allegiance to Sovereign—Most High God—Our Heavenly Father ahead of a respect and reverence for the "king" or the government. Even when unjustly facing death, and dangers, readers are to be ever mindful that the righteous has a promise to expect victory. God shall be our avenger, our defender, our advocate, and all things do work together for good in the lives of the righteous—those who love God.

Therefore, just as this chapter forewarns us, resist the temptation to joy in the trials, tests, calamities, tribulations of the wicked, and so-called enemies, perpetrators, and evildoers. Moving forward from this point, misplaced joyful conduct, when others fall into calamities, can bring forth unintended consequences upon those who fall prey to this temptation and respond accordingly.

A foundation of more than six decades of real-life experiences persuades MrJames to constantly remind himself and all readers who remain engaged in the challenge; that words, thoughts, our daily conduct, and how we apply godly wisdom is significant for positive outcomes in the art of living, and in the reflective blueprint and portrait of your life.

Therefore, Stop—Pause; Listen—Heed; Observe—Do; Think —Reflect; Retain—Remember; this is the roadway to prudence, providence, and divine destiny. There is not a right way to do a wrong thing. To him (her).

29

DAY 25 - PRUDENCE AND DISCRETION

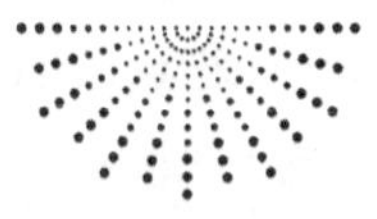

PROVERBS 25

Today is the twenty-fifth consecutive day this month of reading the corresponding numbered chapter from Proverbs; only six more chapters to go and a few more days remaining in the month. An invitation to seek after wisdom titled: "The Art of Living," was issued by MrJames. He asked readers to make a free and voluntary time investment in themselves by asking readers to focus and direct their pursuit of knowledge in the direction of obtaining skillful Godly wisdom; committing themselves daily to read one chapter from The Book of Proverbs—The Book of Wisdom. MrJames has consistently repeated his daily discipline himself for nearly five years.

A thought from MrJames LifeCoach on Proverbs 25:

With increased spiritual awareness, MrJames began reading

this chapter recognizing the personal example set forth by the writers; and acknowledging the value and importance of writing things down. MrJames reminds readers that it was Tom Sawyer who said: “a short pencil beats a long memory” every day.

More importantly, if not for the divine command, and a commitment to writing things down; and concentrated efforts to preserve the Sacred records, the world would not have Sacred Holy Scriptures; because before the existence of Bibles, even the Ten Commandments were written in stone by God himself (Exodus 31:18). More to the point, much of the valuable information that has been passed on to us, down through humanity and from those who came before us, would have been lost to the world.

Reading the 25th chapter this time officially, to make this record, MrJames perceives it is considered wise to write some important things down. Therefore, get out your shovel —pencil and paper; ponder, reflect and review your past experiences, and put to death and bury what Grandma called life f.r.o.g.s.—Frustration—Rejection—Oppositions—Grievances—and Sinful acts; and cast them from your life.

What could be more important to record than the daily unfolding of the events of our divinely created purpose, and to note the important real-life experiences and life-lessons in the art of living and the process of becoming?

What about the relevance and effectiveness of a “Vision Board” that displays your dreams, desires, goals, and righteous aspirations? MrJames believes dreams and goals not written down are merely just fleeting wishes; and in real-life wishes only come true in books, movies, fairy tales, and the miracles of the Make-A-Wish Foundation. Therefore, one message from this chapter is, record your deep-rooted dreams, desires, and goals in writing for a later review; because we never know exactly "what the next day may bring" (Prov. 27:1); and you never know who the reader of your recorded words may be.

It has been said, noted, and evidenced as true: "females write diaries, men write journals" and this chapter, in the wisdom of Proverbs, simply confirms the significance of developing the discipline of journaling as a way to glean insights in the art of living. MrJames believes, intellectually and as a writer himself, that the process of writing engages multiple aspects of higher functions of human capacities and capabilities. Exercising our human ability to write and record our conscious awareness, separates humans from other species, and the process itself, thereby harnesses, bridles, and reins in our divine and human intellect in such a way as to focus us on the specific task at hand.

Likewise, in upcoming future generations, it may be found through research that typing, texting, and keyboarding could produce similar outcomes. Additionally, throughout the Proverbs, writers remind us to "write on the tablet—notebook of our heart—core essence" (Prov. 3:3; 7:3); as their way of implying that we should not just remember these things but also live by them.

Whenever MrJames is writing he finds it difficult, in that present real-life moment; humanly, not just to be fully engaged mentally, but intellectually, physically, emotionally, and psychologically focused as well. He is able to draw from the inner reservoirs of life experiences, knowledge, insights, understandings, and the skillful Godly wisdom that is stored on the tablet of his heart with a concentrated focus and with a singleness of thought.

Reading chapter twenty-five impresses upon me to ask myself: have I intentionally avoided comment on verses that have been repeated, as much as half-dozen times, throughout the Proverbs?" Yes! I must admit.

Since I might just be talking to myself after twenty-five days into the challenge; to my own self I must be true. MrJames, likening instruction of Proverbs unto himself (Matt 11:16-17; 2 Ne 6:5); he acknowledges, takes ownership, recognizes, and he can see that his avoidance of the subject is partly because of the lingering impact of real-life unprocessed pain, and unresolved personal experiences in those matters.

In the words of Grandma and Grandfather Richard; MrJames says to himself and readers: "Baby, come closer YoungMan" and hear the words of this Proverb. While thinking that he was speaking to himself the vibrating sound of Teacher began to permeate his conscious awareness: "MrJames you must need to resist the temptation to avoid looking back to discover, to resolve, and to ponder the life-shattering and life-shaking experiences as you have been doing MrJames; for more than fifty years now."

I could feel concern for my wellbeing coming from Teacher; and simultaneously HE said: "MrJames how are you holding -up? I can feel your pain, so let go, let God and remember f.r.o.g.—Fully Rely On GOD. Remember Bill and Sharon? Before he died from his weak heart, he said to you when Jr Frog died: ***Pain shared is pain lessened; and that's what friends are for*** so sharing of your pain with a friend, brother or sister is the process to release the pain from your life."

Internally, I felt I was filled with ***"joy"*** and seemingly it was as if Teacher had absorbed all my painful memories rooted in events in the past. Then MrJames felt a rushing incoming, relaxing, calming floating sensation. It was as if he was as light as a feather; it felt so authentic, realistic, and genuine. As such, MrJames was so convinced he began looking around for rocks or bricks or anything heavy to put in his pockets so he could keep his feet on the ground.

Apparently aware of my excitement and in a pleasantly pleasing tone, Teacher said: "Pondering past heartaches, hurts, pains, and struggles can be a source for real-life knowledge, real-life insights, and inspiring revelatory impressions that can bring into focus, some concealed and temporarily hidden, but useful life lessons. MrJames, you and readers must need to know that reviewing, reflecting, and "ponderization"—deep intentional reflecting on past unpleasant happenings; can be grueling, emotionally excruciating, and the process will likely be intense."

MrJames was still basking in feelings of elation when Teacher continued: "MrJames warn readers not to be deceived; because by human default the natural—worldly response to genuine, authentic pain is to retaliate, or hide (Gen 3:8), or ***run away*** from the pain; and to run into the direction to find pleasure. Oftentimes, instead of processing through the negative experience, the ***counterfeit artificial feel good sensation*** is looming as the only reasonable, accessible, and undoubtedly the more easily available choice" (Rom 7:21).

However, Teacher continues what is now our longest and most sustained dialog since our initial encounter: "MrJames the doorway leading to divine purpose is found in processing the life experiences. Furthermore, the process can discover and provide meaning, understanding, relief and release; and lead to freedom from bondage and captivity, and possibly negate, minimize, and prevent negative outcomes in the art of living."

Now thinking to himself, MrJames realizes he has been avoiding commenting on some life-controlling issues present in the art of living in his personal life that Proverbs highlights. MrJames can now see the indisputable evidence that the skillful Godly wisdom of Proverbs pointedly suggests that the brandishing truths of Proverbs, are meant to be substituted in place of erroneous acts, actions, choices, decision, and beliefs in the art of living.

MrJames, even now only reluctantly acknowledges, one of the lunging truths in the art of living, that he found to be accurate and descriptive in the Proverbs; but repeatedly he chose to avoid addressing the matter, even in his shared insights. Pondering the thought further, MrJames gains a sense of the potential crippling, debilitating, life-limiting impact, and other life-diminishing effects of failing mindfulness—being present in the construct of reality.

Thinking that he was talking to himself, ushering-in in that present moment was the consciousness of Teacher. Now MrJames knew Teacher was granted privileged access to his thoughts because Teacher began this interaction by saying; "MrJames, yes, it is a terrible situation to be living forty years with an argumentative, quarrelsome, contentious, disloyal, untrustworthy, proud, self-confident- self-righteous and immoral spouse or companion.

Teacher continued with compassion, saying: "MrJames, when mimicking and manifesting, with extreme regularity, these descriptions foreshadow narcissistic personality traits (NPT); you unknowingly have lived with; under the watchful eyes of Guardian Angels, for more than four decades. MrJames, share your thought with Teacher."

Talking as if speaking to Teacher, but inaudible it was to himself: Suffice it to say, MrJames concurs with the wisdom expressed in each verse and cautions readers to take heed to the warnings each of these verses are repeating.

However, the real-life married-life experiences of MrJames are viewed and considered by him to have been beneficial to him. Particularly as the ultimate school of hard knocks classroom; and seen as a treasured chest filled with sacred lessons in the art of living.

Therefore Teacher, MrJames only openly shares deep-digging deeper insights with readers who voluntarily answer the challenge to make a time investment in themselves; and make a daily commitment to read the chapter from Proverbs that coincides with the date of the month. As he concluded his thought, instantaneously, Teacher responded:

"MrJames, that is exactly as the Proverbs instructs. Skillful Godly wisdom only comes from GOD —Eternal realms; and wisdom—SHE must need be valued as important, searched for with a diligence, desired, and pursued with an intended purpose. MrJames, your answer confirms what is known throughout the eternal realms; the secret to unlocking the Godly wisdom of Proverbs is safe behind the eyes and between the ears of MrJames."

Responding to Teacher inaudibly; MrJames thought in his mind: after nearly five years in the process of reading a chapter of Proverbs each day, MrJames is persuaded to acknowledge that throughout the Proverbs there is skillful godly wisdom that is so simple, that readers will fail to understand it because we are expecting art of living insights to be complicated, confusing, complex, and convoluted—opposite of precious, plain, and simple (1 Ne 13:26-29,32,34,40).

However, many of the proverbial teachings relating to daily conduct, speech, attitude, disposition, and relationships are easily understood.

On the other hand, the preferred and recommended list of dos and don'ts within the Proverbs are challenging; and most often can be contrary to natural human tendencies. For example, review verses 21-22 in this chapter and you will find it is suggested not to repay evil for evil but to provide life sustaining sustenance—food when hungry; water when thirsty; to enemies if need be and trust that God will be your avenger. In the art of living, the skillful Godly wisdom of the Proverbs and the true value of real-life personal experiences are priceless, prerequisites and preparatory to our becoming that unto which we were created to become; and as we allow ourselves to be molded to become a reflection of the divine blueprint of our life purpose.

Therefore, MrJames is constantly reminded that readers are invited to be actively engaged in the pursuit and search to acquire knowledge. But not just worldly knowledge and intellect; but with an intentional especial focus on gaining skillful Godly wisdom— "she" must be desired, looked for, pursued, respected, observed, valued, and internalized if we are to produce a life reflective of the blueprint of our divinely created purpose. MrJames remind himself and readers that there is interconnectedness in the disciplines of Science, Religion and Spirituality.

Just at the time MrJames was completing his thoughts to Teacher, the influence of the presence of Teacher grew increasingly stronger; saying: "Baby, YoungMan, MrJames; do not forget the closing words you have felt inclined to end with each day....."

Therefore, God—Our Heavenly Father—Supreme Creator—Master Designer of all that exists "directs our paths" through the choices we make each day. HE is leading us to become what we were destined to become. All we can do is all we can do, after we do all that we can do, trust all things to work together for good so we will accomplish and fulfill our divinely created destiny and purpose; and our life becomes a reflection of the divine blueprint of our created purpose. This is a foreordained, scripted statement, and a message from Eternal realms, Guardian Angels, and Teacher.

In the name of Jesus Christ. Amen.

30
DAY 26 - A MEMORIAL TRIBUTE

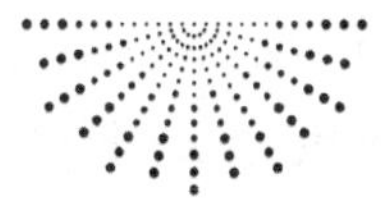

PROVERBS 26

Today is the twenty-sixth consecutive day this month of reading the corresponding numbered chapter from Proverbs; just a few more days remaining in this month, and MrJames knows he might be talking to himself. His invitation to readers to seek after wisdom is titled: "The Art of Living," and it was issued as a way of asking wisdom-seeking readers to make a free and voluntary time investment in their own life. Specifically, he asked readers to focus their pursuit of knowledge in the direction of obtaining skillful, Godly wisdom, by committing to read one chapter daily from The Book of Proverbs—also known as The Book of Wisdom.

Keeping that in mind, "The Art of Living" urges readers to ponder, consider, reflect upon, embrace, and internalize a life-view that accepts a basic core belief of an existence of a Sovereign—All-powerful, All-knowing, Always present;

Most High God in control of all things. However, in the construction of real life, our experiences will include pleasant and not so pleasant tests, trials, tribulations, life-shaking challenges, and unforeseen experiences as well; but not from a religious perspective; from a spiritual perspective.

MrJames views life from the spiritual reality that all real-life experiences are tailor-made with divine purpose, meaning, and valuable life lessons interwoven into the canvas of our life journey.

A thought from MrJames LifeCoach on Proverbs 26:

While reading chapter twenty-six, MrJames immediately began to recognize that there are only a few themes and topics addressed by these twenty-eight verses, especially the first twelve verses. However, all of the verses of this chapter are devoted to the use of vivid and colorful descriptive words, phrases, terms, and comparisons.

Remember, the representatives of the King of Juda felt these verses from Solomon were important enough for them to invest the time to copy them down. It seems the language used was intentional, served to further illustrate and emphasize the potential implication for negative outcomes associated with specific dispositions, attitudes, conduct, and behaviors. MrJames believes the structure of this chapter appears deliberately pointed and descriptive; as are all of the Proverbs when specifically identifying the traits and characteristics of foolishness, self-confidence, insanity, vanity, laziness, good for nothing; and narcissistic foolish personality type.

However, verse two has a different focus and is teaching that unmerited curses do not arbitrarily, ***without rhyme or reason,*** come upon an individual without a just cause (vs 2).

Therefore, it must need be understood, in the art of living there is and always will be a stimulus of causation— cause and effect; sewing and reaping; seeding and planting; followed by a time to harvest that which has been sown. This is an eternal blueprint and outline of the process that produces a curse—undesired empowerment to fail in a situation.

In other words, there is no such thing as a true accident; and nothing ever "just" happens. By the specific use of the word curse in verse two, Solomon's copied words are implying and also explaining that negative outcomes—bad resulting experiences do not just happen, all of a sudden, for no reason whatsoever. Negative consequences do not just rise right out of the clear blue sky, but they are permitted to manifest and come into being by way of cause and effect; but always under the omniscience—all-knowing; and omnipresence—always present awareness and watchful eyes of the Master Designer of ALL that exists.

MrJames is drawn to a place of revelatory reflection as he ponders through this chapter. Thinking to himself, he sensed the presence, and had learned to recognize in his conscious awareness the presence of Teacher. Just as he knew HE was there, the inaudible voice of teacher said: "MrJames, tell them about God—Master Designer of ALL that exists and the first day he said: ***it is not good*** (Gen 2:18). Remember your question you pondered for nearly 10 years? Tell readers about it" and the conscious awareness of Teacher was no longer present.

Exactly twenty-six years ago, in 1998; as I was reading in Genesis for the umpteen time, for the first time reading Genesis I recognized, realized, and internalized in the Biblical accounting of Creation; that the first time God—Supreme Creator said something was not good throughout all the periods of creation, it was in reference to something HE had done himself.

I admit that that revelation of knowledge and insight created total cognitive dissonance within the very fiber of my being. In my mind and heart I knew God as "good" and only doing good. But himself declares having done something I now see as bad. Mind you readers, "come closer" this is important; for 10-12 years I pondered this new found insight while reading and studying inspired writings, different Biblical translations, and praying and fasting for peace and understanding.

Remember, during these years of uncertainty, although I maintained dissonance about the issue, I continued my pursuit for Godly wisdom, knowledge, insight and a deeper understanding about the dilemma in my mind.

However, complicating matters even more during that 10-12 year period of time, from 1996-2000, I became an active addict, entered three residential programs, relapsing a few times, but eventually became a recovering addict, no longer chemically-dependent, but surrounded on one side with a life full of life-controlling issues, and on the other side by mounting doubts and uncertainties in life. To navigate my way through the turmoil of that time, and as a way of escaping my construct of reality; I immersed myself into reading and studying the Word of God, and Sacred other Scriptures.

In 2004, in recognition of the death of my son, I started the 501c3 organization: Real Help Network, Inc. The mission of the organization was focused on educating non-addicted family members about the recovery process, H.A.L.T.—relapse prevention; and early warning signs of life-controlling chemical-dependency.

Additionally, I was serving in a rather highly responsible and somewhat of a spiritually demanding Christian leadership capacity, and this was following shortly after the suicide death of my son; in the midst of the turmoil and uncertainty I was experiencing a life-shaking almost catastrophic business failure; and in 2006, my college bound, favorite (only) daughter became the unwed expecting mother of our first grandchild.

Suddenly, in the midst of this thought, the vibrating inaudible voice of Teacher said: "Tell the readers that life is just a test, and life challenges are intended to steer them to a certain place whereupon the next life lesson will be waiting for them to learn. MrJames you must need to know that some of the readers have been led to this point; go ahead and tell them the best part of my favorite story"....in came a conscious awareness of an ensuring peaceful silence......

There have been previous times, in my life journey; when I have found myself consciously much more aware that I was much more alone, isolated and away from the presence of God. However, this time the distinct difference was that I was also consciously much more dependent on him, than I had ever been before in my entire life. Sitting there that day, 10yrs later, our granddaughter Trinity was nearly a year old.

Moving forward from that point, with that baseline of brief background information as springboard, to understanding the story; readers must need to know that I had already began making notes, writing poems, reading, and studying more with an intentional purpose of publishing a book. On the memorable day referred to by Teacher; I was all dressed in my typical white shirt and business attire. Ready to leave for a meeting, but I was a bit ahead of schedule and too early to leave the house just yet.

It was time for Trinity to be fed, so I put a towel over my chest to cover my shirt and tie, and opened a jar of some Gerber's baby food, it was carrots. I took a little taste for myself first, and quickly decided they were not for me; thinking to myself that those carrots was surely just prepared for baby food.

Amazingly, just as quickly as I had, even at one year old, Trinity had decide she did not like Gerber's carrots after the first taste hit her taste buds. However, thinking to myself, she was the infant; I was the grandfather; and infants must need to eat Gerber's carrots because they are good for them.

Moving forward from that point, being the grandfather who knows what's best; and I thought those carrots was best for Trinity—the infant. Therefore, like many other determined parents and grandparents, under similar circumstances would do; I continued to force another 2-3 baby spoons, full of carrots into Trinity's mouth.

Then, to my total surprise, as I opened her mouth to put one more spoon full of carrots in her mouth, I soon realized she had not swallowed not one more taste of those carrots after her first taste.

Now, with mouth forced opened, every spoon of carrots that I had forced fed and put in this little infant's mouth; she spit right back out; and those orange carrots got all over my white shirt and tie. Instinctively, I started laughing so hard I almost dropped the baby. That was the day I internalized on a deep level and learned as an absolute truth, that you can not get somebody, anybody, or nobody to do anything that they do not want to do; not even an infant.

With a vibrating sensation of pleasantness, and seemingly the presence of laughter, the inaudible voice of Teacher said: "MrJames, know is the time for you to know this as an absolute and true saying: ***a man convinced or even forced***

against his will, is of the same opinion still, even if that man is just an infant." After delivering that message...silence returned...

MrJames remind readers that through all this time, nearly 10 years has passed and nothing had weighed more heavily on his inner mind and sub-conscious awareness than his question of why had God done this thing to Adam, HIS created MAN, that HE later declared as bad.

More to my point of Inner cognitive dissonance; all these years later, even as I type these words in the present moment, I can recall how confused and distraught I was feeling all those years; and even now, the same thought and the seeming to be incongruence, in the structure and foundation of my belief that had plagued me then, immediately rises in my consciousness. During those days I was haunted by the notion: but "God is good" but constantly asking myself: how and why had God done this thing to Adam?

A few days later after Trinity taught me my lesson with the carrots, it just so happened (by happenstance—so to speak); that I was reading in Genesis again, and at that very place where I had been so concerned about, for so many years. As I began reading the words, the picture on the screen of my mind was Trinity and the carrots all over my shirt.

Then I began to perceive in my eyes that I was reading the words "not good" but behind my eyes, between my ears; and in my conscious mind and intellect, I comprehended and equated the words ***not good,*** to mean ***bad;*** instead of just, not good.

Through all those years, in my own mind—leaning to my own understanding (Prov. 3:5), I remained in a perplexed mental dilemma that was not grounded in truth; but in an ill-conceived, erroneous and internalized belief. My dissonance resulted in a firm belief in "God is good" and my natural mind being at war with that truth.

Trinity and the carrots incident taught me that **good**; **not-good**; and **bad**; are three distinctly different descriptions. Although God—Master Designer of ALL that exists declared "It is not good for man to be alone" (Gen 2:8); HE did not say it was a bad thing, just not a good thing.

The carrots were "not good" to the taste, not even to me; but they were not inherently by their very nature "bad" for human consumption. Likewise, the declaration "not good" does not mean bad. Particularly when the initiator or facilitator of the "not good" circumstance is God—Who is Good—Who is Love—and Master Designer of ALL that exists. If it has been allowed into the construct of your reality it must need be received as having an intentional and intended positive and good benefit.

Not good for Adam to be alone, but beneficial in building a one-on-one relationship with God and created MAN. The carrots were definitely not good, but the nutrients from carrots are beneficial to the body. In the art of living and to live life in such a way as to miss Heaven and end up in Hades would absolutely be a "bad thing" to endure.

However, many of the things experienced in the art of living are definitely not good, uncomfortable, and unpleasant: mother killed in domestic violence, death of first born child, a child sent to prison, early death of younger sibling, breast cancer, mental disabilities, cerebral palsy, rape, incest, addictions, natural disasters, unforeseen and unintended traumatic events, and catastrophic events. The list is endless, although none of these are good and pleasant experiences, neither are they inherently bad experiences in the final analysis of the life course; and in the art of living where the rubber meets the proverbial road; the main thing is to keep the main thing the main thing, and stay focused on celestial.

Unpleasant, discomforting, disruptive, life-shaking, life-shattering, and life-altering events and happenings are the reality of many real-life experiences. In hind-sight now, I understand why Teacher said this is his favorite story. In the mouth of babes profound insights of innocent unadulterated truth can come forth. Remember F.R.O.G.—Fully Rely On God; and when you may least expect it, the answers to your most pressing questions my be revealed. In the art of living, is anything really good or bad; or is everything just is what it is; neither good nor bad? You be the judge!

Therefore, unexpected, unintended consequences, according to this chapter, should be viewed as being permitted to happen for a beneficial reason; and with a specific intended and associated purpose. This chapter of Proverbs rounds out its focus referring to some of the possible stimuli that could trigger negative outcomes; and curses in our life journey that hinder our pathway to becoming what we were created to become.

Some of the negative dispositions and behaviors described throughout this chapter, includes but is not limited to: laziness, slothfulness, sluggards, lying, and insincere flattery. This it follows that the curse of negative consequence comes upon those using phony and fake words to express love; haters, whispering talebearers—gossipers and slanderers, deceivers and backbiters, closed-minded quarrelsome individuals; as well as the selfish, and the self-righteous.

Twenty-six days into the challenge and MrJames knows he might just be talking to himself; but this chapter makes it crystal clear, by the words used, to imply and describe those individuals; by using the appropriate proverbial phrase: ***they are their own worst enemy;*** and they are the producers of many of the undesired, unpleasant situations, circumstances, and negative outcomes that manifest in their lives.

In the art of living a fulfilled life, MrJames reminds readers that there is interconnectedness in science, religion, and spirituality; just as there is connectedness in physical existence by cause and effect in the construct of spiritual reality.

Therefore, by way of eternal laws and principles with which Man is yet to fully understand; God—Our Heavenly Father, Our Creator, Supreme Being, and Master Designer of all that exists "directs our paths" through the choices we make each day; and HE is leading us to become what we were destined to become.

All we can do, is in fact, all we can do; and after we do all that we can do, remember **frog—F**ully **R**ely **O**n **G**od for all things to work together for good; so we WILL accomplish and fulfill our divine purpose; and become a reflection of the divine blueprint of our created.

MrJames dedicates

Art of Living:
Lessons from Proverbs
Remember F.R.O.G.
Fully Rely On God

To his birth mother;
Iola Campbell-Conner
1940—1979
She was a victim in a domestic violence incident
lost her life @ 39yrs old; on 7 Nov 1979

MrJames writes Chapter 26 in honor to:
Jr. Frog:
26yr old son:
[Darrell James Campbell, Jr]
1975—2001;

Darrell Jr. completed suicide, 04 Nov 2001, while struggling in his art of living with depression and life-controlling F.R.O.G.S. of life issues. Rest in peace my dear son; you were loved, and your life was well lived; your eternal impact on my life is profound and this world is a bit better for many, as a result of your short 26 years of walking on this planet.

Although you are absent in your body, your spirit goes with me eternally; sometimes in my conscious thoughts and awareness, sometimes as a present subconscious influence, but you will never be completely forgotten, and throughout all eternities you will always be my son.

In the name of Jesus Christ. Amen.

31
DAY 27 - THE MANNER OF HAPPINESS

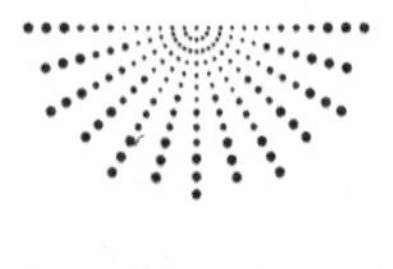

PROVERBS 27

Today marks the twenty-seventh consecutive day, with MrJames: “two or three coming together in Jesus' name” (Matt 18:20), reading and discussing the corresponding numbered chapter of The Book of Proverbs, for the date of the month. I know at this point in the challenge, except for there being a “faithful few,” it could be that MrJames might be talking to himself, even though there are a few more days remaining in the month.

In his invitation for readers to seek after wisdom, titled "The Art of Living," he asked readers to make a time investment in themselves; to focus or direct their pursuit of knowledge on the obtaining of skillful Godly wisdom; and to do so daily, by committing to read one chapter each day from The Book of Proverbs—a.k.a. The Book of Wisdom.

A thought from MrJames LifeCoach on Proverbs 27:

Reading chapter twenty-seven, MrJames feels and believes that it is important to understand, from the writers copied words, that came from the mouth, tongue, and lips of Solomon; why King Solomon chose to use harsh, negative, and degrading words; labels, titles, and descriptions of the wicked as: simple, folly, fool, and foolish. A thorough review of the Proverbs will reveal to readers the high frequency of which these labels are used.

Therefore, a study of The Book of Proverbs has revealed to MrJames a distinct vibrating sound; clear beliefs, actions and behaviors; and a mindset that identifies, describes, and define fools and their foolishness to the consciousness of the readers.

For example: There are specific descriptive indicators and labels for those who ignore, reject, make fun of (mockers), and those who seek not after—self-confident and self-righteous—the counsel of the Supreme Creator—God—Heavenly Father—Master Designer of all that exists.

Furthermore, within this chapter there are various and sundry references in the Proverbs to solidify, clarify, and crystallize the readers understanding of what it means to be labeled a fool or foolish.

MrJames believes one of the primary purposes for writing The Book of Proverbs is to aid the fool and foolish in their pursuit to gain wisdom—skillful Godly wisdom. Therefore, a real challenge to the art of living your life on purpose is the separating of yourself from desiring to be seen as wise according to the world's standards. Oftentimes, the wisdom of the world is but foolishness to the Supreme Creator—God —Heavenly Father—Master Designer of all that exists.

Some more positive and opposite labels used by the writers to describe acceptable ways of living your divinely created purpose is: humble, friendly, wise, diligent, and prudent—to gain and live according to skillful godly wisdom. There are many other topics touched on in this chapter that MrJames has not mentioned.

However, there is another term mentioned a few times in the chapter that MrJames believes is significant and deserves to be paid attention to by those reading this section. The term —friend, friendly, or friendship should be revered, respected and used in a sacred and privileged manner. MrJames feels this way primarily because it is a term used by Jesus in addressing his disciples and followers (John 15:13-15).

Moreover, in the art of living across his more than six decades, MrJames has a multiplicity of personal examples of true individual friends and friendships—Guardian Angels and impactful teachers who taught him, valuable life lesson, by the lives they lived. In the art of living, from these friends, and Grandma he received a first-hand witness of a lives being lived in harmony with skillful Godly wisdom.

As such, these experiences demonstrated true, authentic, genuine examples of friend and friendship as a priceless commodity in the art of living; and the designation of friend and friendship should be held in high esteem in the life journey.

The Godly wisdom revealed in this chapter establishes that all associations, acquaintances, and social interactions are not friendships; and some so-called friendships can be unbalanced, one-side, unreciprocated, selfish, manipulative and deceitful.

However, sometimes difficulty in development and healthy growth of friendships is the interaction of "iron rubbing against iron" and sharpening one another. In other words, the clashing effects of some friends—irons—the wise and prudent, sharpening of each other; may result from becoming better in the art of living, and genuinely striving to become a reflection of the blueprint of a divine created purpose.

This chapter seems to suggest that the wise and prudent ("iron") improve their life chances; their potential to have a harvest of positive outcomes and they become favored. The art of living in divine purpose requires interaction with other individuals on the life journey that are wiser and more prudent. Therefore, it takes iron to sharpen iron; much like the rubbing together of two knives or rubbing a knife on a sharpening stone—whetstone, or honing-steel at the proper angle will sharpen and help to maintain the blades. Therefore, it follows that those seeking skillful godly wisdom, with a desire to live wiser more prudent lives of divine purpose, requires relationships and interactions with "iron" (Prov 27:17).

Therefore, it follows that God—Our Heavenly Father—Our Creator—Supreme Being—Master Designer of all that exists, through the day by day choices we make, "directs our paths" and HE is sharpening, honing, and leading us to become what we were destined to become. All we can do is all we can do, after having truly done all that we can do, trust all things work together for good, and ultimately we are becoming a reflection of the divine blueprint of the created purpose of our lives.

Remember; remember, remember; and do not forget, reading The Book of Proverbs and applying the teachings in the art of living is the roadway to prudence, providence, and divine destiny. There is no other way; and there is also not a right way to do a wrong thing. To him who knows to do right but does it not; to him, it is considered sin (James 4:17).

32

DAY 28 - DARKNESS EXPOSED

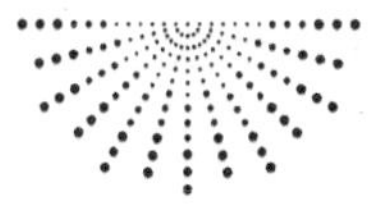

PROVERBS 28

Today is the twenty-eighth consecutive day this month, reading the corresponding numbered chapter from Proverbs. For some readers, there may be only three more days remaining in this challenge this month. Usually, MrJames reads from the King James Bible; however, his insights also come from reading the New King James, New International Version, New Living Translation, and Amplified Classic versions of the Holy Bible.

In real-time and in real life, our experiences will include pleasant and not so pleasant tests, trials, tribulations, life-shaking challenges, life-shattering train-wrecks, and many other unforeseen experiences as well. MrJames views life events not necessarily from religious perspectives but from the spiritual reality that all real-life experiences are tailor-made with divine purpose, meaning, and valuable life lessons interwoven into the canvas of the real-life experience and are intended to be beneficial to the individual on our life journey.

A thought from MrJames LifeCoach on Proverbs 28:

Before I compiled and expressed this thought, I was inclined and prompted to read from three additional translated Biblical versions of this chapter. In my review, I came to see, summarized in all versions, a subject matter in this chapter under three headings: Greed and pride, trust and confidence, and caring for the needy.

Greed is translated as a form of pride—a form of idol worship in some translations—reflected and exemplified in the gimme, gimme, gimme, and the "it's all about me" attitudes. MrJames believes this implies that being greedy, stubborn, self-centered, craving thine own way, arrogant, and seeing oneself in a higher status in comparison to others (narcissistic personality types) are all attitudes—fruit from the same tree.

Each of the mentioned attitudes and behaviors is plainly set forth in Proverbs and is to be avoided at all costs. The negative consequences attached to these dispositions and attitudes that will follow in the passing wake and walk side-by-side with them will be in direct opposition to the art of living a life that is aligned with divine created purpose.

The negative implied connotations associated with being prideful and greedy are sprinkled throughout the Proverbs, and such dispositions always lead to produce an undesired harvest of hard knocks and negative consequences, in the long run. MrJames believes, according to Rev 12:7-10, pridefulness, arrogance, and greed are evil gateway personalities and demonic character traits and could aptly describe the rebellious acts committed in heaven by Lucifer —Satan—Devil before the foundation of creation was ever laid. As such, "God resists the proud, but gives grace to the humble" (1 Peter 5:5).

In one recorded example, MrJames notes; even when the Supreme Creator—God—Heavenly Father—Master Designer of all that exists expressed satisfaction following the completion of each period of creation; according to the blueprint of creation and as recorded in the Book of Genesis; HE only said it was "good," and even at the completion of our created world, HE said: it is "very good," but never once did HE express, nor imply that HE was "proud" of the accomplishment.

In a second example; later-on in Biblical history; noted and recorded in an account following the Baptism of Jesus; the Supreme Creator—God—Heavenly Father—Master Designer of all that exists; for the second time when acknowledging HIS satisfaction, again the only words HE expressed was: "I am well pleased" baring and absent of indications of feeling prideful.

A third fitting example is in the Biblical recorded story of the second introduction of HIS Son, taking place on the Mount of Transfiguration. There said HE—Most High God—The

Creator—Heavenly Father—Master Designer of all that exist; expressing HIS satisfaction, HE only said he was "well pleased" (Matt 17:1-8); and again, HE did not use any words to convey nor imply subtly a feeling of pridefulness. MrJames believes, as is always the case, HIS choice of words was intentional.

Finally, in a fourth recorded Canonized Scriptural account of Sovereign—Most High God—Heavenly Father— Supreme Creator—Master Designer of ALL that exists; introducing HIS Son Jesus Christ to the ancient inhabitants of the Americas; that was reportedly recorded sometime after HIS crucifixion on the cross at Calvary. The voice again spoke from Heaven; in the similar manner, following the same pattern as before; as it has been recorded, and said: "Behold my Beloved Son, in whom I am well pleased, in whom I have glorified my name—hear ye him" (3 Ne 11: 3-7).

In acknowledging his respect for the reference and emphasis on trust in this chapter; MrJames believes it is to establish "who" it is that one should place their trust in. King Solomon, the author of the chapter, does this by stating to readers, using no uncertain terms; how idiotic, foolish, vain and senseless it is trusting in self; describing it as having a deceitful nature. He strongly emphasizes further that being self-confident is the pathway to disaster.

Therefore, MrJames believes the skillful Godly wisdom obtained from reading and study of the Proverbs, and as it relates to the art of living; will persuade, direct, encourage, and incline the wise to live out a divine created purpose; and urge readers to put all trust in the Supreme Creator—God—Heavenly Father—Master Designer of all that exists.

Trust, allegiance, reliance, and dependence on God is the true highway to safety, protection, and deliverance from hurts, harms, and dangers in the art of living. Solomon's words also assure readers, hearers, and doers that there are seen and unseen dangers lurking around and about as we travel our life journey.

Finally, instructions related to caring for the poor suggest, confirm, and highlight the existence of a connection to an abundance of blessings that are promised to those who are mindful to do so. Recorded in the Gospel accounts, Jesus said: "The poor will always be with you" (Mark 14:7). Solomon also instructs: "he who gives to the poor lends to the Lord" (Prov 19:7).

However, this chapter also explains that being poor or needy is not the worst condition to find yourself in. The hard-hearted, the insensitive, those lacking in integrity and empathy, or those with narcissistic attitudes towards others; and even being wealthy can be a worse state than being poor. The humble poor are rich in faith (James 2:5), and the poor in spirit are in right standing to inherit the kingdom of God (Matt 5:3).

Because of the importance and significance of that statement; MrJames believes it deserves and must need be repeated: the humble and poor in spirit are in right standing with God—Supreme Creator—Heavenly Father—Master

Designer of all that exists. As such, he believes one of the primary purposes for writing The Book of Proverbs; is to aid the foolish, the simple-minded, the humble, and those poor in spirit in their pursuit in the art of living to gain wisdom—skillful Godly wisdom. The label used by the writers describing an acceptable way in the art of living a divine created purpose is prudence—to gain and live according to skillful Godly wisdom.

Today, nearly six decades have passed since MrJames read The Book of Proverbs that first time; and after many types of real-life experiences in the art of living, the initial insights he gained have become "10 Absolute Core Beliefs" of his life. MrJames found these beliefs reading, but life itself taught and revealed to him that these beliefs are spiritual truths; he learned from the eternal realms to build upon them; and in the art of living they are the fertile ground to build upon to produce and harvest a life reflective of the blueprint of our divinely created life purpose.

Remember: He who knows and knows he knows is wise. However, he who knows but knows not that he knows is yet still unlearned, immature, and ignorant. He who knows, lives, carries, and conducts themselves—self-mastery, according to that which they know is the wiser. He (she) who learns from his (her) own experiences, the experiences of others, or learns from reading, hearing and hearing (Rom 10:17), and listening to instructions from others, he (she) are wisest.

On the other hand, the fool and foolish learn not from their own experiences; neither the experiences of others, nor learn from hearing and hearing and a Therefore, Stop—Pause; Listen—Heed; Observe—Do; Think—Reflect; Retain—Remember; this is the roadway to prudence, providence, and divine destiny. There is not a right way to do a wrong thing. To him who knows to do right, but do it not; to him it is considered sin (James 4:17)

33
"LOOK-R-HERE" SELF

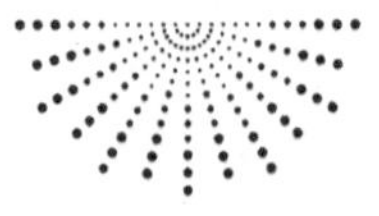

WEEK FOUR

The words of this literary work might just be to myself, owing to the reality of the fact; sometimes I just must need to talk to me. I am saying to me: "Look-R-Here self" and Grandma would be saying: "Baby, come closer." I know that you know, and it has been said: "The two most important days in every person's life are the day they were born; and the day they find out why they were born."

Moving forward, keeping that thought in my mind through the inspiration and revelation of these words, I remind you Self, that the inner desire to know the truth of my divine destiny is coming forth from the eternal realms of our pre-existence. Dr. M.L. King, Jr. describes this overwhelming desire to know, is to be trusted because it is rising from: "the eternal blueprint for my created life purpose." As such, eventually, this truth must needs to be accepted, pursued, embraced, internalized, and applied in the art of living here on the earth. A similar absolute truth was taught by Jesus—TEACHER—Master Designer of All that exists; and it is written and recorded in the Holy Scriptures like this: "Unto whomsoever much [knowledge, revelation, and spiritual insight] is given, much is [entrusted, intended, expected and] required" (Luke 12:48).

MrJames, knowing he just might be talking to himself on this twenty-eighth day of the challenge; realizes these words illuminate, accentuate, and enlighten in him the profound significance of voluntary concentrated efforts to discover what Tom Sawyer profoundly alluded to: "For what purpose came I into this world?" MrJames suggests readers liken that question unto yourself.

Jesus, who is no respecter—not partial to persons (Acts 10:34; Rom 2:11), confirms and affirms the inherent absolute potential for us to know this truth, when HE said: "For this purpose was I born, and for this purpose I have come into the world" (John 18:37).

Oftentimes, in the art of living, I have reflected, studied, and pondered over those words before; saying: "Look-R-Here Self, why was I born?" However, on this 28th day of the challenge, on behalf of readers and listeners, I sense there is a deeper understanding of those words being birthed within the fibers of my being.

Therefore, I voluntarily choose to "Lean not unto [my] own [smartness, cleverness, worldly intellect, human philosophy and] understanding" (Proverbs 3:5), but with sincere gratitude and appreciation, clothed in sackcloth and ashes, humbled with genuine intention in this present moment. Furthermore, I consciously acknowledge the deepening of my understanding of the words of Luke, specifically as they pertain to Self, You, and all other readers, hearers and doers of this challenge.

In honor of Most High God: Our Heavenly Father; Supreme Creator, Master Designer of All that exists; respect for Jesus Christ—God's Son—my personal Savior and Redeemer of All of Mankind; I know in my inner self it is the Holy Spirit —Teacher, Guide, Companion, Protector; the "rod and staff" (Psalm 23:4) that leads, guides, and directs me in the art of living. He is my comforter in life as I journey to become what I am created to become.

I know not why the words resonate so deeply within me, on behalf of readers, hearers, and doers, during this present moment. Nevertheless, I cannot deny the authenticity of feeling a profound deepening of my conscious awareness, spiritual insight, and understanding of association and relationship with elect and select challenge keepers.

Therefore, I cast out any doubts and uncertainty and fully accept into the construct of my reality: the little black boy from Prichard, Alabama; the grandson of James and Sarah Thompson; the son of James Thompson Jr. and Iola Campbell Conner; the adopted son of Richard and Willie Inez Campbell; adopted brother with Glenda and Jacquelyn Campbell is one of the whosoever referenced in Luke 12:48.

In spite of all that, in my inner self, I recognize that I have been curiously aware of special experiences, unique challenges, choice blessings, divine protection, and unmerited Heavenly favor, permeating around and about me, and all throughout my life.

I am reminded of words I often repeat, as a mantra, to Self, and sometimes when with others. These often repeated words are speaking much more louder to me in this present moment, more distinct and penetratingly clearer than ever before; as I transpose and transcribe my thoughts into transcript and manuscript of words. Today, I will read them aloud as if they are to be heard in the eternal realms. These are the words of the mantra:

Look-R-Here, SELF: YOU are One-Of-A-Kind; there has never been another person exactly like YOU—or me, in the history of mankind, nor will there ever be. God, Our Heavenly Father—Supreme Creator, and Master Designer of all that exists; HE has made YOU—and me, One-Of-A-Kind; rare, unique, and valuable. God said it, I just believe it, and that settles it."

Reflecting on my blessed and highly favored life, and the words of Luke 12:48, I consciously acknowledge from behind my eyes and between my ears, I feel so inadequate and undeserving of the unmerited favor. But, truly, I know I have been given much Godly Wisdom, spiritual insights, knowledge, and understanding. Therefore, I seek the companionship of the Holy Spirit to help me along the pathway ahead in the art of living.

Help me!

In the name of Jesus Christ. Amen.

34
DAY 29 - PRAY FIRST

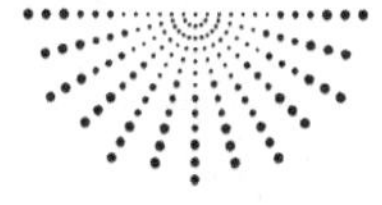

PROVERBS 29

Today, we embark on the twenty-ninth consecutive day of reading the corresponding numbered chapter from Proverbs for the date of the month. There is only one or two more days remaining in the month after today. Readers, hearers, listeners, and doers who stood up for the challenge on day one will have completed four full weeks of answering the challenge. Well done; keep moving forward; and just like a

f.r.o.g. in the tub of buttermilk, you must need to keep-on kicking, kicking, and kicking; do not quit before the miracle.

Get your shovel out to dig your grave for those f.r.o.g.s. And be as busy as a one-legged man in a kick fight; or a one-armed paper hanger in the art of living; and in constructing the canvas of your life journey.

Keep-on Coming Back and Showing-up Do not stop before the miracle (More will be Revealed)

The Christian faith makes It possible for us to accept that which cannot Be changed, to meet disappointment and sorrow with an inner poise, And to absorb the most intense pain without abandoning our sense of Hope, for we know, as Paul testified, in life or death, in Spain or Rome, "that all things work together to them that love God, to them who are the Called according to his purpose."

– Martin Luther King, Jr.

A thought from MrJames LifeCoach on Proverbs 29:

While preparing to make this entry, I was reminded of the frequency the writers of Proverbs has mentioned that the people rejoice when leaders are righteous, and tremble and hide when leaders are wicked. However, Proverbs also indicates the Supreme Creator—God—Heavenly Father—Master Designer of all that exists has made both the righteous and the wicked, loves us all, and is no respecter of persons. Generally, the righteous are associated with consistent goodness, blessings, divine favor, positive expectations, and dependable outcomes. On the other hand, the wicked are associated with calamity, turmoil, temporary gain, instability, negative, undesired, and unintended outcomes.

However, the closing words of this chapter (vs 27) offer what could be understood as an explanation for some of the strife and contention that is present in some human interactions and relationships; in particular, the unequally yoked relationships between the righteous, or the wicked and unjust. The righteous is the enemy of and wars against wickedness; and the insights of wickedness and the wicked is the enemy of and wars against righteousness; and in opposition to the insights of skillful Godly wisdom.

The relationship between the righteous and wicked—the fool and the foolish, is similar to the relationship between oil and water—they do not and are not intended to be mixed. No more than to expect "sweet water and bitter water from the same fountain" (James 3:10-12). A similar warning is heard throughout the Proverbs in relation to the prideful, the selfish, the self-confident; being in partnership with those whose trust is in the Lord.

The primary focus of the combined words of this chapter is on the future vision, the unfolding of the blueprint of the divinely created purpose of our lives. Those with vision and revelations of truth and knowledge of the redemption of God; live blessed—happy, hopeful, fortunate, desirable lives that are absent of the fear of man; but filled with faith, reverence, respect and honor for the Supreme Creator—God —Heavenly Father—Master Designer of all that exists.

Therefore, God—Our Heavenly Father, Our Creator, Supreme Being, and Master Designer of all that exists "directs the paths" of the righteous; and through the choices we make each day HE is leading us to become what we were destined to become. All we can do is all we can do, after we do all we can do we must need to trust all things to work together for good; so we will accomplish and fulfill the full measure of our divinely created purpose; and in the construct of our life canvas we will become a reflection of the blueprint (Jer 29:11) of our divinely created purpose.

Remember: He who knows and knows he knows is wise. However, he who knows but knows not that he knows is yet still unlearned, immature, and ignorant. He who thinks he knows but really knows not, is often foolish, immature, irritating, and can be a nuisance; he will run off him who does know; and can even squelch the Holy Spirit.

Therefore, Stop—Pause; Listen—Heed; Observe—Do; Think —Reflect; Retain—Remember; uprightness is the roadway to prudence—skillful Godly wisdom, providence, and will lead us to our divine destiny. There is no other way; and there is not a right way to do a wrong thing. Thus, "to him who knows to do right, but does it not; to him it is sin" (James 4:17).

35

DAY 30 - AIM HIGH / DON'T QUIT

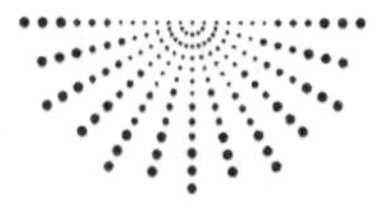

PROVERBS 30

<u>A thought from MrJames LifeCoach on Proverbs 30:</u>

I am consciously aware of the fading away of another month of a year that is slowly passing. The clock continues: tic-toc, tic-toc, tic-toc; the clock never stops, and time goes on. But our limited allotment of time is a precious commodity in the art of living and in our present state of existence. The sand in the hourglass is wasting away silently; out of sight, out of mind; but time is constantly, steadily, and gradually progressing forward; it never stands still, and never moves in reverse.

There are many references in this chapter to a diverse selection of issues addressed within these written words of wisdom attributed to one named Agur. Such as it is, there are some complex, perplexed, perverse, and perturbed things on the earth. In this concluding chapter, the writer includes among these things: the way of adulteress women. In contrast, there are four things too wonderful to be understood fully; and there are four things that are never to be satisfied. There are a few things vividly highlighted and strongly emphasized in the text next to the closing chapter in Proverbs—the Book of Skillful Godly Wisdom.

However, the closing thought of this chapter warns against destructive self-confident acts, individual foolishness, self-righteousness, self-exaltation—prideful self-praise, grandiosity, self-centeredness; and narcissistic personality types. These types of perverted self-worship and praise are akin to idol worship; labeled to be "sparks of an unholy fire" (Isa 50:11); and they should be restrained and avoided at all cost.

Interestingly, Agur uses several comparisons of different animals to explain some dos and do-nots of human behavior; and to expose and highlight some of the mysteries of life. Each animal selected has unique, distinct qualities and characteristics.

Just as I began to fully disclose learned insights from my years of reading this chapter of Proverbs; it was then that I became consciously aware of the incoming presence of Teacher; and as HE arrived He was saying: "MrJames you are not just talking to yourself, and it is not good (Ecc. 6:12) in life and in the art of living, for you to tell them everything; just as Grandma told you, Baby."

I remembered Grandma had given me a similar warning, but seeming as if Teacher new my thoughts and my memories; HE continued within my memory and my thoughts: "The reason why I, Teacher and Grandma said that to you is because some things must need be learned from Guardian Angel Experience itself; some things must need be learned from Guardian Angel Hardknocks; some things must need be learned from Guardian Angel Knucklehead; but all things has an appointed time (Ecc 3:1-8); there are assigned tutors to each student in the art of living; when the student is ready the teacher will appear; this is an absolute law of life; eternally established, governed, and controlled from the eternal realms of existence."

Detecting a sensation of compassion; Teacher continued: "however, the narcissistic—proud, fool, arrogant, selfish, self- centered, calloused, spiritually insensitive, idle, lazy, slothful, and scornful—these kinds—demonic influences only become wiser but through prayer and fasting (Matt 17:21). MrJames, you may attempt to discipline, teach, guide, instruct, and talk until you become blue in the face; but only Sovereign –Most High God—Supreme Creator—Master Designer knows how, where, and when to intervene; and that is in the due timing appointed within the eternal realm….." Although now Teacher had departed from my conscious awareness; in my mind and within my innerself I realized that Teacher knew I understood; even more intently now, the instructions given by both of them; Teacher and Grandma.

As I continue my insights on this chapter; I do so under self-restraint from full disclosure; but with that guardrail in-place I proceed to highlight just a few of the noted animals referenced in this chapter. However, I choose to leave the bulk of them for readers to ascertain for themselves, with assistance from the eternal realms: Animals such as: Eagle—greatest soaring bird (Isa 40:31); Lion—king of wilderness(1 Peter 5:8); Ants—industrious (Prov 6:6-9); and a male goat—insensitive leader (Matt 25:32-34; 41-43); just to name a few, but I feel confined by the eternal realms from going any further. Therefore, I say no more.

Purposefully, with real authentic and genuine intent; instructed to do so, MrJames has only briefly mentioned a few of the passages from this chapter. However, his desire to encourage readers to open The Book of Proverbs and read, especially this chapter in particular, is of an utmost importance in his conscious efforts to convey to readers, listeners, and remaining doers who continue to stand-up to the challenge.

With all that has been said and the implied relevance to readers; Is there need for King Solomon, Agur, Grandma, Grandfather Richard, Teacher, or MrJames to say any more? The primary focus of the combined words of the final three chapters are focused on the future vision, and on the unfolding of the blueprint of the divinely created purpose of our lives.

Persons with visions and revelations of truth; and with knowledge of the Sovereign—Most High God— Heavenly

Father, Supreme Creator, Master Designer of ALL that exists; and who accept HIS Plan of Redemption; Plan of Happiness; and Plan of Salvation of God are portrayed to live blessed—happy, hopeful, fortunate, desirable lives. An existence that is characterized by the absence of the fears of man; but filled with faith, reverence, respect, praise and honor for God—Supreme Creator—Heavenly Father—Master Designer of all that exists.

Skillful Godly Wisdom is a female—reproductive; and "she" must be desired, looked for, pursued, respected, observed, valued, and internalized if we are to conceive and produce a life reflective of the blueprint of our divinely created purpose. Remember, the intentions and objectives of MrJames, through the art of living challenge is to introduce readers, hearers, and listeners to holding themselves to a better way to live. The art of living is to be focused fully on living life as a reflection of the preordained blueprint of the divinely created purpose of your life as being wise and prudent.

In the art of living the full measure of a fulfilled life, MrJames LifeCoach reminds readers that there is interconnectedness in science, religion and spirituality. Therefore, God—Our Heavenly Father—Our Creator—Supreme Being—Master Designer of all that exists "directs our paths" in and through the choices we make each day. HE is leading us to become what we were destined to become.

The Main Thing is to Keep the Main Thing the Main Thing.

All we can do is all we can do, after we do all we can do, trust that all things do work together for good, and we will accomplish and fulfill our divinely created purpose; and become a reflection of the preordained blueprint of our divinely created purpose.

Remember: He who knows and knows he knows is wise. However, he who knows but knows not that he knows is yet still unlearned, immature, and ignorant. Therefore, Stop—Pause; Listen—Heed; Observe—Do; Think—Reflect; Retain —Remember; this leads to the way of to prudence, providence, and divine destiny.

There is no other way; and there is not a right way to do a wrong thing. To him who knows to do right, but do it not; to him it is considered sin. Too soon old, and too late smart. Are you getting Wiser, or just getting older? To thine own self, will you be true?

God knows our thoughts no matter who or where we are. "O LORD, you have searched me and known me! You know when I sit down and when I rise-up; you discern my thoughts from afar" (Psalms 139:1–2). God searches the hearts and minds of people, seeking those whose hearts are turned to Him (Jer 12:3; Acts 15:8). Thoughts are the most private part of our human experience. No one, no other person can know our thoughts unless we communicate them; so, we tend to feel, imagine, and fantasize anything that we think is considered safe if it stays only in our minds.

But, there is ONE—Most High God who always knows what we are thinking, why we are thinking it, and HE knows the motive behind our thoughts (Prov 20:27). I know I might just be talking to myself; but there are times when I do not even know my own thoughts, myself; and, oftentimes I do not know why I am thinking what I am thinking. However, God knows not only our thoughts, but HE knows everything about us; and HE is omniscient—knows everything about everything.

Congratulations, being well pleased I tip my hat in salute of readers, listeners, and doers for the diligent follow-through on your time commitment and investment in yourself. If your start was day one of the challenge, then you have completed 30 consecutive days reading from the Book of Skillful Goodly Wisdom.

Therefore, I know greater insights of knowledge, understanding, prudence and wisdom in the art of living will be yours as you continue to habitually immerse yourself into The Book of Proverbs. As we are walking through the Proverbs, crossing over the threshold into the final chapter, preparing to exit this monthly challenge; stop, observe, think, retain; and hopefully you will begin anew.

As you pause to review and reflect; I suggest to readers, hearers, listeners, and doers to ask yourselves: Are you getting Wiser or just getting Older in the art of living? Remember, that a half-truth is a whole LIE. Therefore, to thy own self, will you be true?

36

DAY 31 - STAY FOCUSED, CELESTIAL

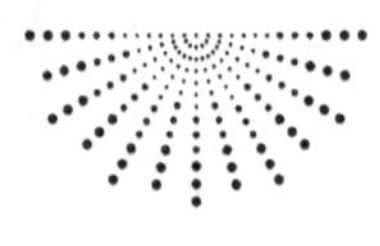

PROVERBS 31

A thought from MrJames LifeCoach on Proverbs 31:

Remember, most of the words of wisdom recorded in The Book of Proverbs came through Solomon. However, as pointed out previously, these final three chapters are recorded by different sources. It is feasible to think that these writers are recording these eternal words of wisdom as a way to preserve other important sayings being passed down through ages but possibly had not been written down and recorded. It could be that King Solomon is also the primary source of this wisdom.

On the other hand, particularly as it relates to this final chapter, these recorded words are expressed and attributed to a mother's instructions and teachings to her son. MrJames view them as real-talk from a mother keeping it 100%; keeping "erry'thang-erry'thang;" calling a spade a spade; a pure and unadulterated birds-and-the-bees talk about the art of living.

It is obvious to MrJames that the words of the mother to her son, who is a king, are sincere, heartfelt, genuine, authentic, filled with love, passion, and commitment. Such that her words are delivered unapologetically in a manner that illuminates them with an implied belief that her words are eternal, irrevocable, unalterable, and everlastingly true.

There is an undeniable connection between living the abundant life; as promised and designed by the Supreme Creator—God—Heavenly Father—Master Designer of all that exists; and our chosen spouse and eternal life-companion. MrJames offers this caution to all readers, hearers, and listeners: do not become dismayed, perplexed, or confused when reading this chapter; thinking the words are single in focus; only directed and applied to the woman —female—she.

Sovereign—Most High God—Heavenly Father—Supreme Creator—Master Designer of ALL that exists; is no respecter of persons (Acts 10:34-35). Therefore, these instructions apply equally true for the opposite gender—man (he, him) as well. If in fact the man—male—him—he acts and conducts himself in a manner descriptive of “she” as recorded in this chapter, the outcomes will be the same. Consequently, the adulterer, the lazy, the adulteress, he or she who may sleep and slumber; he (she) who walks not in strengths of dignity, prudence, and skillful godly wisdom shall also come to ruin.

Therefore, these words of caution, warning, and instruction against these activities and conduct are equally applicable to both genders; can bring extreme consequences and f.r.o.g.s. into the pathways of life, and annoy, spoil, and confuse the art of living. Thus, the described acts highlighted by this mother: are able to alter, detour, or hinder the life course pathway of becoming what we were created to become, and thereby frustrating, obstructing, and marring the real-life reflection of the blueprint of our created purpose.

From a foundation of over six decades of real-life experiences, MrJames reminds readers that "knowledge is power" and words, thoughts, our daily conduct, our use and application of godly wisdom is significant in determining positive outcomes and progression in the art of living. Therefore, as a LifeCoach, he is constantly reminding listeners to actively engage in the pursuit and search to acquire knowledge; especially skillful godly wisdom— "she" must be desired, looked for, pursued, respected, observed, valued, and internalized if we are to produce a life reflective of the blueprint of our divinely created purpose.

Remember, those original primitive insights of twelve-year-old LifeCoach, was nearly six decades ago; after many real-life experiences in the art of living, today they have become "10 Absolute Core Beliefs" of his life. LifeCoach found them to be eternal truths upon which to build a life reflective of the blueprint of our divinely created life purpose.

In the art of living the full measure of a fulfilled life, LifeCoach reminds clients that there is interconnectedness in science, religion, and spirituality. Therefore, God—Our Heavenly Father—Our Creator—Supreme Being—Master Designer of all that exists "directs our paths" in and through the choices we make each day. HE is leading us to become what we were destined to become.

All we can do is all we can do, after we do all we can do, trust that all things do work together for good ... I think I feel the incoming presence of Teacher, but he is not coming alone this time. I can feel multiple familiar influences and they are overwhelming my sense of conscious awareness. It seems that I am using much energy attempting to form words to speak. Immediately, in the midst of that thought, the presence of Teacher was there.

I became aware of the overwhelming presence of the many Guardian Angels that are assigned to assist me in the art of living journey of becoming a reflection of the blueprint of my created purpose. I knew it was for some reason they were all there; some were family members, relatives, friends, classmates, co-workers, church members, business partners, educators, and some were casual strangers I met on the streets.

However, through a familiar but inaudible form of communication, I was unmistakably informed: "TEACHER is now the constant art of living influencer of my life, sent from the eternal realms, and at my beckoned call; responsible to assist me on my journey; and if necessary, HE is authorized to literally take me by hand to lead, guide, and navigate my steps around f.r.o.g.s. of life, detours, roadblocks, and the pitfalls on the pathway to the next phase of enlightenment in the art of living journey "

Without warning, but preceded by a vibrating and increasing crescendo sound of a trumpet, I perceived in my inner-self an authorized, solemn, official, but inaudible voice—more like a vibrating feeling than a sound; and TEACHER said: "MrJames, you have done all that you can do; the student is ready; you kept the main thing the main thing; and with the close of this chapter you have completed the required six years of daily reading a chapter from Proverbs. You are one of the few to have voluntarily done so; therefore, now you are revered as Guardian Angel LifeCoach; and will be recognized as such in the eternal realms."

Left feeling the weight and responsibility of being LifeCoach, I received this message from the eternal realms: "Remember LifeCoach, the Guardian Angels are at your beckoned call as needed, and you have become the inaudible Guardian Angel LifeCoach to all readers and to whomever who answers the challenge; you are rare and unique, just as the blueprint in the eternal realms reflects; and your real-life experiences are valuable to others in the art of living. This attraction is fulfillment and manifested reality, according to the mantra you have consistently repeated into the eternal realms many times."

Through the fading presence of TEACHER, it was made known to me: "You must need know that only a few have been so diligent to be renamed in the art of living and labeled LifeCoach from the eternal realms. Therefore,

TEACHER must need be sent to reveal to you; there is, built-in and inherent with this accomplishment; the forthcoming of new insights and deeper understandings; and a further deepening of connection into the eternal realms. Moving-on from this point, the source of infinite intelligence related to 10 Absolute Core Beliefs will be revealed to you; and they are to be shared with all readers and hearers; and especially those who voluntarily answer the challenge....

Then LifeCoach sensed the presence of Grandma: "Baby we are so pleased that you are now acknowledged in the eternal realms, and in the art of living, as LifeCoach. It must need be Grandma was sent to reveal that you have entered a sacred space of divine intervention in the art of living. As LifeCoach, you have been granted Angel Infinite Intelligence, who will shore-up and strengthen you along your way from the eternal realms; and who is source of the 10 Absolute Core Beliefs that were revealed to you. Angel Infinite Intelligence is to assist you in building and constructing a present reality that will be a reflection of the preordained blueprint of our divinely created purpose.

Remember: He who knows and knows he knows is wise. However, he who knows but knows not that he knows is yet still unlearned, immature, and ignorant. Therefore, it is wise to make time in the art of living to Stop—Pause; Listen—Heed; Observe—Do; Think—Reflect; and then Retain—Remember. There is not a right way to do a wrong thing. To him who knows to do right, but do it not; to him it is considered sin. Are you getting "Too soon old, and too late smart?"

Congratulations, I tip my hat and salute readers and the clients for your diligent follow-through on your time commitment and investment in yourself. I know greater insights, knowledge, understanding, and Godly wisdom; in the art of living, will be yours as you continue to habitually immerse yourself into The Book of Wisdom.

Today, again we walk through and cross over the threshold as we exit one month, and prepare to begin anew; LifeCoach is asking readers, clients, and MrJames to ponder and reflect on the question: Are you getting Wiser, or just getting Older on your journey to become that unto which you were created to become? To thine own self, will you be true?

Finally, at the end of the proverbial day, "where the rubber meets the road" spiritual acceptance and healthy contentment will come as we embrace life circumstances as was instructed centuries ago in a poem titled Desiderata, a copy was given to me as a gift nearly fifty years ago.

In hindsight, I can see this message was sent directly to me from God—Heavenly Father, Supreme Creator, Master Designer of all that exists— and it describes that there are real-time, real-life challenges, and present-day life lessons to be learned while here on this life plane we call Earth. As time progresses, I am imagining myself leaning forward without any doubts, and accepting the words of the poem: "the universe is unfolding as it should, and it is still a beautiful world."

I am furthermore reminded that at the end of the periods of creation, in Genesis it was recorded by Moses that God looked out over our newly created world; and proclaimed not that it was good, as HE had stated several times before; but it was recorded that HE said it was "very good" (Genesis 1:31). God—Our Heavenly Father, Supreme Creator, the Master Designer of all that exists said the world HE had created was very good; I just believe it, and that will settle it for LifeCoach.

However, on this final day of the month of the challenge; consumed with thoughts of the upcoming insights to be revealed from eternal realms by Angel Infinite Intelligence; and related to 10 Absolute Core Beliefs; I know I might just be talking to myself.

In the name of Jesus Christ. Amen.

37
DAILY ROUTINE

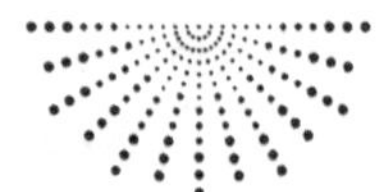

28 DAYS FORMULA FOR CHANGE

Commitment I

Daily, for 28 days, seven days a week (before 7:00 am), read 1 Chronicles 4:9-10 [Prayer of Jabez]; read Deut 28:1-14 [Blessing for Obedience]. You may choose to repeat this process for three cycles (84 days). Insert your name and read or memorize the Words in first person, present tense: e.g. "And Jason is more……" e.g. "If Devin fully obeys."

Commitment II

Daily and continuing for 28 days, seven days a week (before 7:00 am), read Isaiah 54; and 3 Ne 22). You may choose to repeat this process for three cycles (84 days). Insert your name and read the Words in the first person, present tense: "Enlarge the place of Glenda's tent……"

Commitment III

Daily, for 28 days, seven days a week (before 9:00 am), read Isaiah 40:28-31; and Isaiah 55:6-13. You may choose to repeat this process for three cycles (84 days). Insert your name and read the words in the first person, present tense: "…my thoughts are not Jessica's thoughts…."

Commitment IV

Daily, for 28 days, seven days a week, for at least 84 consecutive days, read the Chapter from Proverbs that coincides with the date of the month (calculate your end date, set reminders in phone calendar, on bathroom mirror, refrigerator, or etc.). Going forward, consistently repeat this discipline on a daily basis. If today's date was the 15th and this is your first day accepting the challenge; read Proverbs Chapter 15. Tomorrow read chapter 16; the next day read chapter 17; and so on…. Liken the words unto yourself as you read. Every day going forward, pray first; aim high (you may choose to read chapter 2-3x day), stay focused and prioritize reading one chapter from Proverbs at least once each day. Repetition and consistency are critical and important in the art of living. As a practical exercise: place your hand over your chest to feel The constant beating of your heart. Keeping this in mind: LifeCoach believes there is an eternal beneficial essence to repetition of some things in life.

The famed heart surgeon, Dr. Thomas S. Monson explained: "When you continue to do some thing [anything] repeatedly, that thing will become easier to do; it is not that the thing gets easier to do, but [it is that] the power [and desire] to do that thing gets stronger" like exercising a muscle.

In applying that principle to the challenge; the thing or the muscle is your consistent repetitive exposure to Proverbs, or to reading any Sacred Scriptures and writings will bring forth increased insight and understanding of skillful Godly wisdom.

Commitment V

Twice Daily, at least for 28 consecutive days; mid-day, evening, or just before bed; read the section that is titled "Look-R-Here SELF" from chapter 33 of this volume. When reading this before bed, read the words aloud with feelings and emotions, preferably before the stroke of midnight, because in these last days, midnight is the official start and beginning of a new year, and of each never-used-before new day.

Commitment VI

Daily, consistently for 28 days, seven days a week for at least 84 consecutive days, repeat and recite aloud at least one verse from the chapter of the day read from Proverbs. Repeat and declare this mantra to yourself:

"Going forward I will prioritize my day."

First—offer a prayer of gratitude for a brand-new never-used-before Day; and further prioritize your prayer time to be completed before getting fully dressed, before coffee, before Facebook, before emails; before—during—or as a part of breakfast. Prioritize into your conscious awareness the importance of praying before your day begins, and before leaving the house.

Second—Declare this mantra to yourself:

"I will make my bed before leaving my room"

At the very least I will do it before departing away from the house for the day. Your resolve to make your bed before leaving the house is an assurance and commitment to hold yourself accountable to yourself; so that no matter how the day may unfold; you will always be greeted, reminded, and encouraged at the end of your day by at least one task you completed, or at the end of each day you can always add to other completed task of the day: A made-up bed is sure to bring a smile to the face of most mothers across the world.

Third—Declare to yourself:

"I will end my day with prayer"

Pause to ponder, review, and reflect on the happenings of the passing day; forgive and ask forgiveness for any offenses, resolve any f.r.o.g.s. in interactions with others; and express gratitude to: Most High God—Our Heavenly Father, Supreme Creator, Master Designer of ALL that exists.

Commitment VII

Make a commitment to fasting; and fast from food and drink for at least one day (24 hours—two consecutive meals) each month. During your period of fasting; read, memorize, or recite Luke 12:48 a minimum of seven times; read the Proverbs chapter for the day once again; and read Isaiah 58 entirely during your period of fasting. Be mindful to maintain an attitude of a present conscious awareness, and hopeful expectation of personal Godly intervention and insight in the art of living to be forthcoming in the "due timing of the Lord" (John 7:6); and the good, acceptable, and perfect will of the Lord (Rom 12:1-2) be manifested "on Earth as it is in heaven" (Matt 6:10).

Additionally, LifeCoach specifically recommends reading the prayer titled "God Memorandum" by Og Mandino. Other suggested books by Og Mandino includes: The Greatest Salesman in the World; The Greatest Salesman in the World Part II: End of Story; The Greatest Secret in the World; The Greatest Miracle in the World.

If readers seek additional insights; LifeCoach recommends

reading Celestine Prophecy by James Redfield.

House of Frogs

Everybody Frog, Somebody Frog, Anybody Frog, and Nobody Frog; all had an important thing that needed to be done. Everybody Frog was asked to do it; but Everybody Frog was sure Somebody Frog would do it; since Anybody Frog could have done it, but Nobody Frog did not actually do it. Somebody Frog got angry because it was important to Everybody Frog. Everybody Frog thought Anybody Frog could do it, but Nobody Frog realized that Everybody Frog would not do it. Therefore, it ended up that Everybody Frog blamed Somebody Frog, when Nobody Frog did not do what Anybody Frog could have done.

AFTERWORD

Closing thoughts from MrJames LifeCoach:

In my six decades of real-life experiences, I have come to realize that gradual, consistent, concentrated efforts may seem outdated in the construct of present world reality of smartphones, microwaves, text messages, and email.

However, in spite of the potent saturation and influence of those things; and although we do live in a quick paced microwave construct world of reality—I want it yesterday mentality: not a right now, but a "rat" now demanding society; and even though all knowledge on the planet has been placed literally at our fingertips;—just ask Google—your decision to stand up and answer the challenge to make a daily incremental time investment in yourself will be eternally profitable.

Searching for skillful Godly wisdom in the art of living by

investing small daily increments of exposure to Proverbs—The Book of Wisdom; and other Sacred Holy Scriptures is a decision that may provide you the greatest residual and an everlasting eternal return on an investment from any other strategic investment decision you may make in the art of living (Proverbs 2:2-6; 3:13-16).

LifeCoach suggests that readers acquire and gain access to a personal journal to begin a permanent record of your personal experiences with The Book of Proverbs and the Scriptures for your later review, reflection, and as a testimony and legacy for descendants and relatives who will come after.

Remember, remember, remember! "Life is lived forward, but life is understood backwards" (C.S. Lewis). As readers take the time to reflect, review, and ponder experiences from the past; as LifeCoach, I pray that God will bless your "sincere, real, and intentional" (Moroni 10:4) efforts, and whatsoever you "put your hands to will prosper" (Deut. 28:8).

Experience may be the best TEACHER, but oftentimes it is also the most expensive. The smart man learns from his own mistakes. The smarter man learns from the mistakes of others. The educated man learns from books, research, and evidence-based theoretical reasoning. The wisest man listens to wise council, learns from his own mistakes, the mistakes of others, and from listening to and applying skillful Godly wisdom in the art of living.

Nevertheless, the wisest man learns from his mistakes, the mistakes of others, things he reads in book, hands-on experiences, the real-life experiences of others, through original thought, through revelation, and by divine inspiration.

However, the immature fool, the foolish, the self-confident, and non-empathetic narcissistic brutes learn not from their own experiences, nor from the examples and experiences of others, neither from stories, books, parables or Proverbs; nor from the School of Hardknocks University, or from traveling the wilderness of A #1 Knucklehead Academy.

Such as some may be; because on the final analysis, at the end of the day; and where the proverbial "rubber meets the road" of progression, in the art of living "there are such unfortunates, they seem to have been born that way" (AA—Big Book; Prov 30:2).

In the pages of: ***Art of Living: Lessons from Proverbs—Remember F.R.O.G.*** is where MrJames, Grandma, TEACHER, and LifeCoach will ask readers and hearers the ancient, age old question: "Where are you?" (Gen 3:9). To thine own self be true.

In the name of Jesus Christ. Amen.

www.ingramcontent.com/pod-product-compliance
Lightning Source LLC
LaVergne TN
LVHW041015150826
845672LV00001B/97